trattoria

Michael Roulier wishes to thank his assistant Stefan Hoareau.

Emmanuel Turiot would like to thank the following people and stores for lending their props: Home autour du monde, Blanc d'ivoire, Galerie Sentou, Mise en demeure, Au fond de l'allée, Le Bon Marché, Habitat, The Conran Shop, Derrière le rideau, Axis, La Grande Épicerie, Françoise Le Boulenger, Établissements Poletti, Palladio, Mélodies Graphiques, Deux Mille et Une Nuits Aude Freixo-Turiot, Le Printemps, Institut culturel italien.

The editor wishes to thank Édouard Collet, Christine Martin and Mélanie Joly for their valuable aid and Marine Barbier for her careful reading.

casual italian cooking at home

trattoria

Isabelle Sensi

Photographs by Michaël Roulier
Design by Emmanuel Turiot

[When the flavors blend…]

To everyone's delight, national borders are slowly disappearing in matters of cuisine. As the new century gets underway, we're witnessing a gradual acceptance of culinary habits from other lands. We don't talk about "exotic cuisine" anymore because exotic means far away and unfamiliar. We no longer consider Chinese, Indian or Mexican food to be strange fare. The sources of inspiration for our cooking no longer matter as long as the results are delicious. It used to be that trying our hand at foreign cuisine was considered audacious, daring, but today it's part of our everyday lives. Ingredients that, in the past, had to be tracked with the skill of a detective or brought back by traveling friends, are now available locally from the neighborhood supermarket or our corner grocer. We are no longer intimidated by spices, mysterious jars, or colorful fruits — instead we are learning how to use them. The world is coming into our homes and its diverse flavors are being awakened in our kitchens. At the same time, we're discovering different ways of eating and new dietary principles. Our kitchens have become the melting pot for a natural blending of tastes; what was once unusual is now so familiar that we forget it has foreign origins.

Small tables covered with white tablecloths, happily crowded together on a plaza or on the street. Flowers casually placed in a pitcher, and bread served while you wait—this is the trattoria—the Italian version of the bistro. In a joyful and relaxed setting, you can find trattorias serving the best cuisine from different regions in Italy. There are the fried artichokes of Rome and the pastas from the South, their aromas melding with those of Venetian seafood, and their colors in vivid contrast to the white truffles of Umbria. The reputation of some trattorias goes beyond the borders of their neighborhood. Travelers can savor specialties prepared "like nowhere else in the world." While pizza has traveled around the globe, the delights of the trattoria have been kept more secretive: Their welcoming environment and excellent culinary skills form the attraction. There is no great mystery in the success of the Transalpine tavern: the freshness and quality of the produce, simple and honest preparation, friendly service, cohesiveness of a family tradition (trattorias are often family businesses) and the culinary know-how and understanding of food and its preparation. Italian food never seems to be as good as it is in Italy, yet we can easily reproduce the flavors at home with careful selection of ingredients. There are numerous specialty stores and good Italian products that are easy to find. They may be a bit expensive, but so delicious that it takes very little to create a great Italian dish.

contents

antipasta

antipasta

to wake up
the palate

Italy has raised hors d'oeuvres to a high point of refinement. Antipasta is

generally served in small quantities so as not to ruin the appetite. These little dishes

of food are a charming way to introduce the delights that are to follow. They include

little fried meat pies, rustic bread, homemade pickled vegetables, mushrooms,

or fish preserved in a little vinegar and olive oil. You can find great varieties of

antipastas in jars at local grocery stores or specialty stores, or you can easily

make your own with simple ingredients from your pantry and/or refrigerator.

**Crostini of Gorgonzola
with mascarpone**
Serves 4–6
Prep time: 10–15 minutes

5 ounces Gorgonzola
3 tender ribs celery
1 apple
1 lemon
1 baguette
2 tablespoons
   chopped walnuts
Pepper

[assortment of crostini]

Crostini with fresh figs
Serves 4–6
Prep time: 15 minutes

6 fresh ripe figs
1 baguette
Olive oil
5 ounces Parma ham,
  thinly sliced

Crostini with anchovies
Serves 4–6
Prep time: 15 minutes

4 ounces salted
  anchovy fillets
2 cloves garlic
5 sprigs fresh parsley
Freshly ground pepper
4 tablespoons olive oil
1 tablespoon
  balsamic vinegar
1 baguette
4 hard-cooked eggs

Crostini of Gorgonzola with mascarpone: Crumble the cheese with a fork. Chop the celery finely, cut the unpeeled apple in very thin slices and sprinkle them with lemon juice. Slice the bread in half horizontally, then in small diagonal pieces and toast them. Spread each one with cheese and sprinkle celery; add a slice of apple and some nuts. Sprinkle with pepper.

Crostini with fresh figs: Peel and crush the figs with a fork. Slice the bread in half horizontally, then in small diagonal pieces and toast them, and sprinkle with a little olive oil. Place a bit of the ham on the toast and spoon some of the crushed figs on top of the ham.

Crostini with anchovies: Soak the anchovies for 15 minutes in a bowl of water. With your fingers in the water, carefully separate the fillets and rinse them. Peel the garlic, and rinse and dry the parsley. Place the garlic, parsley and anchovies in a blender, add pepper to taste, and process until smooth. Add the olive oil and mix until creamy; add the vinegar and blend. Slice the bread in half horizontally, then in small diagonal pieces and toast them. Place a slice of hard-cooked egg on each round before spreading it with the anchovy spread.

[eggplant hors d'oeuvres]

Serves 6
Prep time: 30 minutes
Resting time: 1 hour
Cooking time: 30 minutes

3 large oriental eggplants
3 medium-sized tomatoes
Salt
8 tablespoon olive oil
6 ounces mozzarella
   cheese
2 branches fresh basil
   (about 12 leaves)
Pepper
A few drops
   balsamic vinegar

Wash and cut off the ends of the eggplant. Rinse and dry the tomatoes. Cut each eggplant into 4 slices, lengthwise, about ½ inch thick, after removing some of the peel (see picture). Sprinkle with fine salt and allow the eggplant to drain for about 1 hour.

Rinse and dry the eggplant slices well, using paper towels. In a big frying pan heat some of the olive oil and add the eggplant slices. Cook in batches, adding more oil as needed, until they are golden and tender. Remove them and place them on paper towels to drain. Let them cool off. Slice the mozzarella cheese into 12 slices and the tomatoes, across, into 4 slices each. Wash and dry the basil leaves. Arrange 2 eggplant slices crosswise on a plate; in the center place a slice of tomato and sprinkle with salt and pepper, follow with 1 basil leaf, 2 slices of mozzarella, 1 basil leaf and, finally, a slice of tomato. Sprinkle with salt and pepper to taste. First, fold over the two ends of the bottom slice, then the other two and fasten it all together by putting a toothpick through it.

Continue in this manner with the other eggplant "bundles." Arrange them on an oiled pan and bake them in a preheated oven at 350°F for 30 minutes.

When ready to serve, warm or cold, sprinkle 2 drops of vinegar over each bundle.

[mixed seafood fry]

Ask your fish market to clean the calamari and save the tentacles, and fillet the drum fish. Cut the calamari into ½ inch rounds and drop them in 1¼ cups water in a saucepan, to which the milk has been added. Poach them for 30 minutes. Remove with a skimmer and drain. In the same broth, poach the shrimp for 5 minutes. Drain and shell them.

Cut the drum fish in small cubes. Mix the ingredients for the marinade and pour the marinade over the cubes of fish. Let it marinate for 1 hour.

Prepare the batter for the fritters: In a salad bowl, mix the flour, ¼ cup water, the beer and a pinch of salt. Add the 1 tablespoon of oil and let it stand for 1 hour. Just before cooking the fritters, gently blend 2 egg whites (beaten stiff) into the batter. In a deep fryer, heat the oil to 375°F.

Take the fish cubes out of the marinade and dry them on paper towels. By turns, dip the calamari, shrimp and fish cubes in the batter and then drop them into the deep fryer—not too many at a time. Fry them for about 5 minutes. When they are a nice golden color, drain them and serve accompanied by lemon wedges, and a mesclun salad (see page 92) with olive oil.

In the same manner, you can prepare a mixed vegetable fry replacing the seafood with cubes of celery root, 2 inches long, rounds of unpeeled baby squash, broccoli flowerettes, squash blossoms, or sage blossoms dropped raw into the batter. Serve warm, sprinkled with a little lemon juice.

Serves 6
Prep time: 30 minutes
Cooking time:
about 35 minutes
Marinating and resting
time: 1 hour

1¼ pound calamari
(about 5 inches long)
1 pound firm fish (such
as drum fish, sea bass
or grouper)
½ cup milk
1 pound medium-sized
shrimp

For the marinade:
Juice of ½ lemon
6 tablespoon olive oil
2 tablespoon mixed
fresh herbs (thyme,
oregano, parsley)

For the batter:
1 cup sifted flour
4 tablespoons light beer
Salt
1 tablespoon oil
2 egg whites
Oil for frying

[mushroom turnovers]

Serves 6
Prep time: 30 minutes
Cooking time: 15 minutes

10 ounces firm fresh
   mushrooms
2 tablespoons olive oil
1 clove garlic
3 ounces ricotta cheese
1 egg
1 pound freshly grated
   Parmesan cheese
15 fresh mint leaves
   (small to medium in size)
Salt and pepper
2 sheets frozen puff pastry
   (17-ounce package)
1 egg yolk
Butter for baking pan

Carefully wash the mushrooms and slice them thinly. Put them in a hot frying pan with the olive oil and shake or stir constantly. Peel and crush the garlic and add it to the mushrooms, but don't allow garlic to burn.

Once the mushrooms have lost their moisture, remove them from the heat and mix them with the ricotta, the whole beaten egg, the Parmesan cheese, and the chopped mint until the mixture is well-blended. Add salt and pepper to taste.

Unroll the pastry sheets. Using a 2-inch cookie cutter, cut 16 rounds out of each sheet.

Place a level tablespoon of filling in the center of half of the rounds. Then cover them with the remaining rounds. Press the edges of the pastry with moist fingers to seal them, and press edges lightly with a fork.

Preheat the oven to 350°F. Decorate the top of each turnover with a scrap of pastry and brush it with the beaten egg yolk.

Arrange the turnovers on a buttered baking pan and bake them for 15 minutes. Serve warm.

[dried tomatoes]

Makes about 3 jars
Prep time: 15 minutes
Cooking time: 3 hours
Curing time: 3 days

5 pounds small ripe
   tomatoes (Roma or plum)
Oil for baking pan
Coarse grain salt
Dried oregano
⅔ cup olive oil

Wash tomatoes and cut in half length-wise. Remove the seeds and the juice by pressing with your fingertips.

Put the tomatoes close together on an oiled baking pan, cut side up, and sprinkle with salt. Cook them in a warm oven (about 170°F) for about 3 hours. They will dehydrate and dry.

Transfer them to sterilized jars, add a pinch or two of oregano; press them down and cover them with olive oil.

Cover the jars and keep them in a cool, dark place; cure for 3 days before using. They may be kept for up to 2 months.

[dried tomatoes
on puff pastry]

Unroll the puff pastry sheets and keep them on their paper. With a 1½- to 2-inch cookie cutter, cut out 16 rounds. Line a baking pan with aluminum foil and oil it. Place the pastry rounds on the foil and press the center of each round to make an indentation.

Preheat the oven to 400°F. Cut the mozzarella in thin slices. Purée the tomatoes and their oil. Spread each round with a bit of mashed dried tomatoes.

Top it with a slice of mozzarella and press down again (to reduce rising in the center of the rounds. Sprinkle with salt and pepper and oregano, and drizzle a little olive oil over the tops. Bake them for about 13 minutes. When the tarts are ready, sprinkle some chopped basil on the melted mozzarella and serve immediately.

Serves 4–6
(makes about 16 tartlets)
Prep time: 10 minutes
Cooking time: 13 minutes

1 sheet frozen puff pastry,
  defrosted (17-ounce package)
Oil for baking pan
2 ounces mozzarella cheese
⅓ cup sun-dried or oven-dried
  tomatoes in oil
Salt and pepper
3 pinches dried oregano
Olive oil
A few leaves fresh basil

[eggplant preserves]

Makes 2–3 wide-mouthed jars
Prep time: 30 minutes
Cooking time: 5 minutes
Resting time: 1 hour
Marinating time: 12 hours.

4 eggplants
Salt
⅔ cup white vinegar
1 small green bell
  pepper, sliced
4 cloves garlic,
  peeled and halved
2 teaspoons peppercorns
Salt
1½ cups olive oil,
  more if needed

Wash the eggplants, cut off the ends, and peel. Cut them in slices ½ inch thick, sprinkle with salt and let them drain in a colander for 1 hour.

Bring to a boil 2 quarts of water with the vinegar. Rinse the eggplant slices and drop them in the boiling liquid. Cook them for 2 minutes after the liquid resumes boiling. Drain them carefully.

In a bowl, gently mix the eggplant slices, bell pepper, garlic and peppercorns. Adjust the salt, cover with olive oil and let marinate in a cool place overnight.

Next day, distribute the eggplant with bell pepper and the peppercorns into previously sterilized jars, pack them down and cover with olive oil. Close the jars tightly.

The preserves will keep for at least 2 months in the refrigerator.

[fricassee of
young artichokes]

Rinse the artichokes; cut off the top portion of the tough outer leaves. With a pointed knife scrape the leaves as if sharpening a pencil. Cut off the tops (see photo). Cut the artichokes in halves or quarters, depending on their size.

Peel the shallots and the garlic. Chop the shallots and slice the garlic finely. In a large frying pan, heat the olive oil and fry the shallots for 2 minutes. Add the artichokes and the garlic, salt and pepper. Brown artichokes for 2 minutes over high heat. Reduce heat.

Sprinkle with the white wine and the thyme and simmer for 10 minutes. The artichokes should be a bit crunchy. Enjoy them, warm or cold, sprinkled with chopped parsley.

Serves 6
Prep time: 15 minutes
Cooking time: 10 minutes

3 young artichokes
3 shallots
3 cloves garlic
6 tablespoon olive oil
Salt and freshly
  ground pepper
½ cup dry white wine
1 sprig fresh thyme
2 tablespoons chopped
  fresh parsley

[stuffed zucchini
with almonds]

Wash the zucchini and cut off the ends. Cut them in half lengthwise. With a pointed knife held at an angle, scoop out about ½ inch of the flesh from each half and reserve it.

Soak the bread in the milk. Beat the egg and add the reserved zucchini flesh, finely chopped, to the egg with the Parmesan and basil. Press and drain the bread and add it to the mixture. Mix until well-blended. Add salt, pepper and the almonds.

Put the zucchini halves on an oiled baking pan. Stuff them with the filling and drizzle with olive oil.

Bake for approximately 35 minutes in a preheated 350°F oven, until the zucchini is golden.

Serves 4
Prep time: 15 minutes
Cooking time: 35 minutes

4 medium-sized zucchini
4 slices bread, with
  the crusts on
½ cup milk
1 egg
1 ounce Parmesan cheese
1 tablespoon chopped
  fresh basil
Salt and pepper
2 tablespoons
  slivered almonds
Olive oil

Tomatoes are used below to hold a delicious Mediterranean preparation composed of eggplant, capers and pine nuts. Choose ripe tomatoes to heighten flavors.

[tomatoes stuffed
      with ratatouille]

Serves 6
Prep time: 20 minutes
Cooking time: 30 minutes

2 medium-sized eggplants
4 tablespoons olive oil,
    divided
4 tender ribs celery
2 onions
15 tomatoes
15 pitted black olives
1 tablespoon capers
    in vinegar
1 tablespoon pine nuts
1 tablespoon chopped
    fresh basil
1 tablespoon raisins
1 tablespoon sugar
Salt and freshly
    ground pepper
1 tablespoon
    balsamic vinegar
Olive oil for drizzling

Wash the eggplants and cut off the ends. Cut the eggplants in small cubes. Heat 3 tablespoons of the oil in a large skillet and sauté eggplant cubes until soft, for 10 minutes, stirring often. Turn off heat, but leave eggplant cubes in the skillet. Cut the celery in thin slices. Peel and chop the onions. Plunge 3 of the tomatoes in boiling water for a few seconds; cool them, peel, and coarsely chop.

In the remaining oil, brown the celery and the onions over low heat for 8–10 minutes. Stir in the chopped tomatoes, the black olives cut in half, the capers, the pine nuts, the basil, the raisins and the sugar. Stir to blend well.

Pour over the eggplant cubes and add salt and pepper. Stir over high heat for 1 minute. Lower the heat, add the vinegar, cover the pan and continue cooking over low heat for about 10 minutes, stirring often.

Cut the remaining 12 tomatoes in half crosswise, squeeze them gently to get rid of the seeds and the juice, and stuff them with the ratatouille. Serve on small plates with a bed of salad greens and drizzle with olive oil. Serve the rest of the ratatouille on the side.

[mushrooms marinated in vinegar]

Serves 6
Prep time: 15 minutes
Cooking time: 2 minutes
Refrigeration time: 8 hours

1 pound mushrooms
1 lemon
⅓ cup white vinegar
1 bay leaf
1 sprig fresh thyme
1 clove garlic
2 tablespoons olive oil
2 teaspoons salt
Chopped fresh parsley
(optional: bay leaves,
thyme sprigs)
Olive oil for drizzling

Clean the mushrooms and rinse them quickly. Grate the zest from the lemon. Squeeze the juice from the lemon. Put the mushrooms in a bowl and sprinkle them with the lemon juice.

In a saucepan, bring to a boil ⅔ cup water with the vinegar and the spices, crushed garlic and olive oil. Let boil for 1 minute and immediately pour over the mushrooms. Add salt, sprinkle with the lemon zest, cover, and let cool before refrigerating. You may serve the mushrooms a few hours later or the next day; however, they will keep in the refrigerator for up to three days.

To serve, drain, put on a plate, garnish with the herbs and drizzle with olive oil.

[anchovies marinated in lemon]

Serves 6
Prep time:
20 minutes
Marinating time:
6 hours.

1 pound fresh anchovies
2 cloves garlic
1 bunch fresh parsley
1 teaspoon dried oregano
¼ cup olive oil
Juice of 2 lemons
Salt and pepper

Scale the anchovies and remove the insides. Cut the fish in two, leaving the backbone on one side. Cut off the head and the backbone. Quickly rinse the fish and dry them. Peel and chop the garlic, rinse the parsley and chop it. Mix garlic and parsley with the oregano. In a terrine, alternate a layer of anchovies with a layer of the parsley mixture.

In a small bowl, mix the olive oil with the lemon juice, salt and pepper, and pour it over the anchovies. Let it marinate, refrigerated, for 6 hours. Serve as an hors d'oeuvre or starter with toast.

[stuffed calamari]

Ask your fish vendor to prepare the calamari, keeping the tentacles. If using frozen calamari, defrost them first. Chop the parsley, the peeled garlic and the tentacles (if you use the frozen calamari, take two of the pockets and chop them as a substitute for the tentacles). Mix parsley, garlic and tentacles in a bowl, adding the whole egg, the bread crumbs, grated Parmesan and coarsely chopped shrimp. Mix well, adding a generous amount of pepper and a pinch of salt.

Rinse the calamari pockets and stuff them with the mixture. Secure them by inserting a wooden toothpick through each one.

Heat the olive oil in a large skillet and brown the calamari on all sides. When they begin to turn a nice color, deglaze the pan with the white wine. Let it simmer, covered, over low heat for 5 minutes. Continue cooking for 15 minutes longer, uncovered, until the wine has almost completely evaporated. Serve immediately.

Serves 4
Prep time: 20 minutes
Cooking time: 20 minutes

1¾ pounds fresh calamari,
   or 1¼ pounds frozen
   calamari
3 sprigs Italian parsley
2 cloves garlic
1 egg
¼ cup bread crumbs
2 tablespoons
   grated Parmesan
½ pound shelled shrimp
Salt and pepper
⅓ cup olive oil
⅔ cup dry white wine

[stuffed peppers with tomatoes and anchovies]

Wash the bell peppers. Cut them in half and remove the seeds. Wash and cut the tomatoes in halves, and put one half of each tomato inside each bell pepper half. Distribute the crushed garlic over the bell peppers and top with 1 anchovy.

Preheat the oven to 400°F. Place the stuffed bell peppers on an oiled pan, sprinkle with bread crumbs and put one drop of Tabasco sauce over each one. Drizzle with the olive oil. Bake for 35 minutes until they are slightly brown. When they are ready, sprinkle them with chopped parsley.

They can be eaten, hot or cold, as a main dish or on a platter of antipasto.

Serves 4–6
Prep time: 10 minutes
Cooking time: 35 minutes

4 small red or yellow bell
   peppers, the size of
   a lemon
4 Roma or plum tomatoes
2 cloves garlic, crushed
8 anchovy fillets in oil
Oil for baking pan
A few bread crumbs
Tabasco sauce
4 tablespoons olive oil
1 tablespoon chopped
   fresh parsley

For the tapenade: Rinse the capers in cool water and dry them on paper towels. In a food processor or blender, chop the olives with the capers, thyme, olive oil, lemon juice and pepper to taste.

Heat the oven broiler. Place the bread slices on an oven tray and sprinkle each one with ½ tablespoon of the olive oil. Brown them lightly on each side (about 4 inches from the broiler). Cut the tomato in half. Rub each toast with garlic and then with the cut tomato. Spread the toast with the tapenade.

Serves 4
Prep time: 15 minutes
Cooking time: 2 minutes

For the tapenade:
4 ounces capers in vinegar
8 ounces black or green
   pitted olives
1 teaspoon fresh or dried thyme
⅓ cup olive oil
Juice of 1 lemon
Pepper

6 big slices bread, cut in half
6 tablespoons olive oil
1 fresh tomato
2 cloves garlic

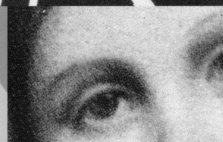

[bruschetta and tapenade]

Bruschetta is culinary art in its simplest form—a simple slice of bread rubbed with olive oil. But what a treat! The bread must be first quality, preferably the crusty, rustic Italian or French-type bread. Carpaccio, which gets its name from a famous Venetian painter, has been popular outside of Italy for more than twenty years.

[assortment of carpaccio]

Carpaccio of beef fillet : Wrap the fillet of beef in aluminum foil and put it in the freezer for 1 hour. Cut it in very thin slices and put on a platter. Mix the olive oil, lemon juice, salt and pepper and pour over the meat. Place it in the refrigerator for 15 minutes. When ready to serve, decorate it with the Parmesan, shaved in thin slivers with a paring knife and the basil.

Veal carpaccio with rosemary: Chop the rosemary leaves very finely and mix it with the lemon zest and olive oil. Cover it and let macerate overnight.
Next day, place the meat for 1 hour in the freezer before cutting it in fine slices. Put on a platter, cover with the marinade, sprinkle with salt and a few turns of the pepper mill. Decorate with the arugula and the cherry tomatoes.

Tuna carpaccio with garlic and peppers: Macerate the bell pepper cut in half (or the dried ones cut open) in the olive oil overnight.

Next day, peel the garlic, rinse and dry the parsley, and finely chop both. Sprinkle over the tuna, and add salt and pepper. Mix the oil from the bell peppers with the lemon juice and drizzle it over the tuna (use bell peppers for another purpose).

Carpaccio of beef fillet
Serves 4–6
Prep time: 10 minutes
Freezing time: 1 hour
Refrigeration time: 1 hour

1 pound beef fillet
⅓ cup olive oil
Juice of 1 lemon
Salt and freshly
  ground pepper
2 ounce wedge Parmesan
  cheese
2 tablespoons dried basil

**Veal carpaccio
  with rosemary**
Serves 4–6
Prep time: 10 minutes
Maceration time: 12 hours
Freezing time: 1 hour

4 branches fresh rosemary
Zest of 1 lemon
½ cup olive oil
1 pound veal
  (underpart of the leg)
Fine salt and freshly
  ground pepper
A few arugula leaves
Cherry tomatoes

**Tuna carpaccio with
  garlic and peppers**
Serves 4
Prep time: 10 minutes
Maceration time: 12 hours

1 fresh red bell pepper,
  or 3 small dried ones
½ cup olive oil
2 cloves garlic
1 small bunch fresh parsley
14 ounces fresh tuna,
  cut in small pieces
Fine salt and pepper
Juice of 1 lemon

[ricotta fritters]

Serves 4–6
Prep time: 10 minutes
Standing time: 1 hour
Cooking time: 5 minutes

1 cup fresh ricotta
2 eggs
2 tablespoons flour
2 tablespoons chopped
  fresh chives
2 tablespoons chopped
  fresh parsley
4 tablespoons capers
  in vinegar
1 teaspoon salt
Pepper
Oil for frying

Crumble the ricotta with a fork in a bowl. Add the whole eggs, flour, chives, parsley, capers, salt and some pepper. Let it stand in a cool place for 1 hour.

Heat the oil for frying (350°F). Carefully drop tablespoons of the batter into the hot oil. They should not touch. Turn them so that they brown evenly, for about 5 minutes. Drain the fritters on paper towels and serve them immediately.

Accompany with a mesclun salad (see page 92), tossed with olive oil and lemon dressing. These fritters make an excellent entrée, or complement to a platter of antipasto.

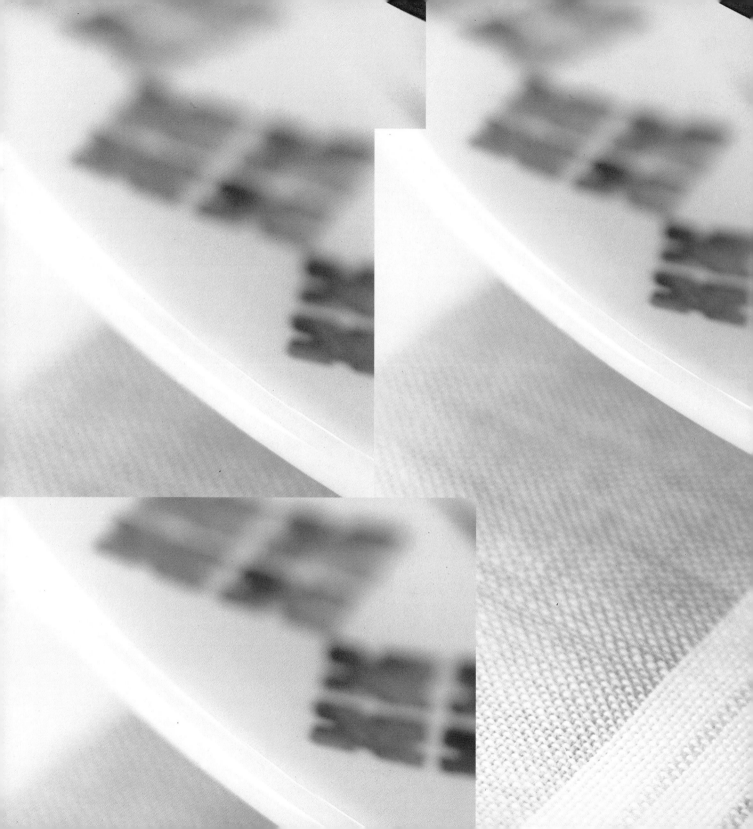

pasta, rice & gnocchi

pasta, rice & gnocchi

indispensable
pasta

What would Italy be without its different varieties of pastas, made of flour, semolina, colored with spinach, tomato, red pepper or even the ink from cuttlefish? Pasta has become a culinary symbol throughout the world. We must also remember Italy's rice, the noble Arborio or carnaroli from the plains of the Po. Only these varieties, prepared correctly, make smooth and creamy risotto.

Serves 4
Prep time: 20 minutes
Cooking time:
about 8 minutes

A handful of raisins
8 anchovies in oil
4 cloves garlic
1 pound broccoli
¾ pound penne
Salt
A handful of pine nuts
⅓ cup olive oil, divided
A few drops Tabasco sauce
1 cup bread crumbs

[penne with broccoli and anchovies]

Plump the raisins in a bowl of warm water. Chop the anchovies and the garlic. Wash the broccoli and separate into flowerettes. Cook flowerettes with the penne (for as long as the package recommends) in a pan with salted water.

In the meantime, sauté the chopped anchovies with the garlic and the pine nuts in 2 tablespoons of the olive oil, for 1 minute.

Drain the broccoli and the penne, which should be *al dente*. Put them on a plate with 2 tablespoons of the olive oil, a few drops of Tabasco, the anchovy purée and the drained raisins. Toss well.

Brown the bread crumbs for 1 minute in the remaining oil, sprinkle them over the pasta and serve. In this recipe, the bread crumbs are a substitute for Parmesan cheese.

[risotto with saffron]

Heat the chicken broth. Take out 2 tablespoons of the broth and soak the crushed saffron in 2 tablespoons of the broth. Wash and chop the onions and, in a large skillet or saucepan with a heavy bottom, sauté onions in 2 ounces of the butter, over low heat, for 3 minutes. Add the rice and let it brown lightly, stirring constantly. Add the white wine and let it simmer until the liquid is reduced by one half.

One ladle at a time, add warm broth to the rice, stirring often. Repeat this as soon as the liquid has been absorbed. After 10 minutes, add the saffron with all its liquid. Cook for about 16 minutes until the rice is *al dente* inside and creamy on the outside. Continue adding the broth until finished. Remove from the stove and add the remaining butter and grated Parmesan. Stir carefully and serve right away.

Serves 4
Prep time: 15 minutes
Cooking time:
about 20 minutes

5–5½ cups chicken broth
½ tablespoon saffron
2 large onions
8 tablespoons (1 stick)
  butter, divided
2 cups Arborio rice
  (12 ounces)
5 cups white wine
4 ounces freshly grated
  Parmesan cheese

[fried risotto balls with ham and mozzarella]

Mix risotto or cooked rice with the eggs and the Parmesan, and add salt and pepper. Cut the ham and mozzarella in small pieces. In the palm of your hand, put a spoonful of the rice (using about ¹⁄₁₂ of the rice). Using your fingers, press a few pieces of ham and mozzarella into it (again, using about ¹⁄₁₂ of the ham and cheese).

Close the rice to envelope the ham and cheese and shape it into a round ball. Roll these risotto balls in bread crumbs. Keep them cool or cook them right away. Drop them in hot frying oil and cook for about 5 minutes until they are golden brown. Drain and serve with a mesclun salad (see page 92) or fresh tomato sauce (see page 60).

Serves 6 (makes about
12 risotto balls)
Prep time: 30 minutes
Cooking time: 35 minutes

2 cups leftover risotto or
  cooked Arborio rice
2 eggs, beaten
2 ounces freshly
  grated Parmesan
Salt and pepper
2 ham slices
3 ounces mozzarella
Bread crumbs
Oil for frying

[lasagna with dried mushrooms]

Put the dried mushrooms in a bowl with 2 cups of warm water and let them soak for 15 minutes. If necessary, clean the bottom of the mushrooms and remove any tough parts. Filter the liquid through a coffee filter and let it settle for 15 minutes.

Sauté the chopped shallots in 2 tablespoon of the butter, over low heat, for 5 minutes. Add the drained mushrooms and cook for 2 minutes. Add the filtered liquid, cover the pan and simmer for 15 minutes. Remove the mushrooms, reserving 1¼ cups of the liquid, and place 1¼ cups of the liquid back into the pan.

Prepare the béchamel by melting 4 tablespoons of the butter; then add the flour and stir for 1 minute. Pour it into the liquid from the mushrooms, and whisk to prevent lumps (if lumps form, beat the sauce, vigorously, by hand or with a mixer). Pour in the milk and let the sauce cook slowly for 5 minutes, until the béchamel coats the back of the spoon. Remove from the heat, add the fresh cream and nutmeg, and salt and pepper.

Preheat the oven to 350°F. Butter a rectangular baking pan, and cover the bottom with a layer of béchamel followed by a layer of pasta strips. Pour a second layer of béchamel, and add a layer of mushrooms, and sprinkle with Parmesan. Continue by alternating layers of pasta and mushrooms. Finish by covering with the remaining béchamel and sprinkle the top with Parmesan. Bake it in the oven for 30 minutes. If you use dry, packaged pasta, then let the pan sit for 1 hour before baking in the oven.

Serves 6
Prep time: 30 minutes
Resting time: 15 minutes
Cooking time: 30 minutes

3 ounces dried mushrooms
3 large shallots
2 tablespoons butter

For the béchamel sauce:
4 tablespoons butter
½ cup flour
1 quart milk
½ cup cream
1 pinch nutmeg
Salt and pepper

About 20 fresh
   lasagna strips
4 ounces freshly
   grated Parmesan

Serves 6
Prep time: 25 minutes
Refrigeration time: 1 hour
Cooking time: 5 minutes

1½ pounds fresh
  or frozen spinach
2 tablespoons butter
2 cups fresh ricotta
2 pinches nutmeg
Salt and pepper
4 eggs
1 cup flour
4 ounces freshly
  grated Parmesan
Flour
2 tablespoons olive oil
Butter for baking pan

For the sage butter:
10 tablespoons butter
  (5 ounces)
15 fresh or dried
  sage leaves
Salt and pepper

[green gnocchi]

Trim and clean the spinach in running water. Put it in a pan with 3 tablespoons water, cover it and cook for 5 minutes (if frozen cook for 15 minutes). Drain and squeeze well; after the maximum of water has been squeezed out, you should have about 14 ounces of spinach.

Put the spinach back in the pan, with the butter. Break up the spinach with a spoon. Add the ricotta, the nutmeg, salt and pepper, and cook over low heat for 3–4 minutes, stirring constantly. Remove from the heat and add the eggs, one at a time, followed by the flour and the Parmesan. Mix it all together well and let it rest for at least 1 hour at room temperature.

Using a teaspoon, scoop small balls of the mixture and shape each to the size of a hazelnut (if desired, each gnocchi may be shaped with the aid of a fork to give it ridges). Roll them in flour.

Preheat the oven to 325°F. Bring a large amount of water to a boil with salt and olive oil. Drop in the gnocchi, a few at a time. When they are cooked, they rise to the surface. Remove them immediately onto a buttered baking pan. Keep them warm in the preheated oven, while preparing the sage flavored butter (see page 40 for the recipe).

[spaghetti with lemon sauce]

Clean the lemons with a brush and warm water, peel off the zest and cut in very fine strips. Plunge the strips in boiling water for 3 minutes and drain. In a small saucepan, melt (do not cook) the butter, add the crème fraîche and stir. As soon as it starts to boil, remove from the heat and add the juice from ½ lemon, the blanched zest, and some salt and pepper. Cook the pasta *al dente* and drain it well before pouring the sauce over it. Mix well, and sprinkle with the chopped parsley and grated Parmesan.

If you wish to serve spaghetti as a main dish, increase the quantities as follows: 1 pound of pasta, 6 tablespoons crème fraîche and the juice of 1 lemon.

Serves 4
Prep time: 10 minutes
Cooking time: 10 minutes

2 lemons
4 tablespoons butter
4 rounded tablespoons crème
  fraîche or mascarpone
Salt and pepper
10 ounces spaghetti
2 tablespoons chopped
  Italian parsley
Freshly grated Parmesan

[potato gnocchi]

Serves 6–8
Prep time: 30 minutes
Cooking time: 35 minutes

3–3½ pounds
  baking potatoes
2 eggs
Salt
2 cups flour
Butter

Wash potatoes and boil in a large pot of water for 30 minutes. Peel them while warm and mash with a potato press. Mix in the eggs and salt. Little by little, add the flour until you obtain a rather firm dough.

Divide the dough into 10 portions and shape each portion into a roll about 1½ inches in diameter. Cut each of the 10 rolls into equal sections, about 1½ inches long, then roll each gnocchi in flour (if desired, each gnocchi may be shaped with the aid of a fork to give it ridges).

Preheat the oven to 325°F. Drop the gnocchi in a large pot of boiling, salted water, 6 or 7 at a time. As they rise to the surface, drain well and put them on a buttered plate. Keep them warm in the oven, while preparing a tomato sauce. (see page 60).

[bolognese sauce]

Serves 6
Prep time: 15 minutes
Cooking time: 40 minutes

1 onion
1 carrot
1 rib celery
1 clove garlic
3 ounces slab
    smoked bacon
3 tablespoons olive oil
12 ounces ground beef
4 ounces sausage meat
½ cup red wine
½ cup broth
4 tablespoons tomato purée
14 ounces peeled
    canned tomatoes
1 teaspoon dried oregano
Small amount of sugar
2 pinches ground cinnamon
Salt and pepper

Rinse and finely chop the onion, carrot and celery. Peel and crush the garlic. Cut the bacon into small pieces and cook in olive oil in a sauté pan. When the bacon begins to brown, add the chopped vegetables, and stir for 1 minute over high heat. Add the garlic, ground beef and sausage meat, and cook for 3 minutes, while breaking up the meat with a fork. Pour in the wine and the broth, add the tomato purée and peeled tomatoes, oregano, sugar, cinnamon, salt and pepper.

Bring to a boil and simmer, covered, for 40–60 minutes over low heat until the sauce coats the back of a spoon. If it seems too thin, finish cooking it uncovered; if it is too thick, add some water.

This spaghetti sauce can be used to prepare lasagna dishes with a light béchamel sauce.

[sage flavored butter]

Prep time: 5 minutes
Cooking time: 3 minutes

8 tablespoons
    (1 stick) butter
15 leaves fresh or
    dried sage
Salt and pepper

In a small pan melt the butter with the sage leaves, until butter is walnut colored and the leaves are a bit crisp. Add salt and pepper to taste. Pour immediately over gnocchi, ravioli or other pasta.

In the same manner, you can flavor butter with rosemary leaves, adding two crushed garlic cloves late in the cooking (don't allow garlic to brown).

The following variation of lasagna will delight all pasta and seafood lovers. Parmesan cheese is optional—some Italian cooks omit it with fish. A white Friuli wine would be an ideal accompaniment.

[seafood lasagna]

Serves 6
Prep time: 40 minutes
Cooking time: 30 minutes

For the court-bouillon:
Oil
1 carrot, chopped
1 shallot, chopped
1 brunch fresh thyme
1 bay leaf
Small bunch fresh parsley
Salt
1¼ pounds fresh
  salmon fillets
3/4 pound white fish
1 pound fresh mussels

For the béchamel:
4 tablespoons butter
⅓ cup flour
⅔ cup crème fraîche
Juice of ½ lemon
4 green onions
1 tablespoon butter
20 fresh lasagna strips
½ pound shelled shrimp
2 tablespoons chopped
  fresh basil
1 ounce Parmesan cheese

Prepare the court-bouillon: In a large pan, heat the oil and brown the chopped carrot and chopped shallot. Pour in 6 cups of water, add the herbs and some salt. Boil for 5 minutes and then drop the salmon and white fish into the court-bouillon. After it returns to boiling, remove from the heat, and let the fish poach for 3 minutes. Take the fish out, and remove the skin and any bones. Save the court-bouillon. Clean the mussels and put them in a covered pan with a bit of water, over low heat, until they open. Shell them and add their juice to the court-bouillon. Filter court-bouillon through a coffee filter. There should be 5 cups of court-bouillon.

Prepare the béchamel: Melt the butter and whisk it with the flour for 1 minute. Then add the court-bouillon, in small amounts, whisking constantly to prevent lumps. Cook at a slow boil, for 5 minutes, until the béchamel coats the back of the spoon. Remove from the heat, and add the crème fraîche and the lemon juice.

Peel the green onions, leaving some of the green part, and brown them in butter over low heat. Preheat the oven to 350°F. Butter a dish and coat the bottom with béchamel and then put a layer of lasagna strips, do not leave any spaces. Cover with béchamel followed with layers of small pieces of fish, mussels, shrimp, onions and basil. Continue in this manner until you have 4 layers of pasta and 3 layers of seafood. Finish with a layer of béchamel and sprinkle with Parmesan cheese. Bake for 30 minutes and serve.

[crêpes with spinach and ricotta]

Serves 6
Prep time: 45 minutes
Resting time: 1 hour
Cooking time: 45 minutes

For the crêpes:
1¾ cups flour
3 eggs
¾ cup milk
¾ cup beer
2 tablespoons oil
1 pinch salt
Butter for cooking crêpes

For the filling:
1¾ pounds frozen spinach
1 pound fresh ricotta cheese
2 eggs
6 ounces Parmesan cheese
1 pinch freshly grated nutmeg
Salt and pepper

For the tomato "coulis" (purée):
1 onion
3 tablespoons oil
14 ounces diced canned tomatoes
2 tablespoons tomato concentrate
1 clove garlic
1 branch fresh thyme
6 ounces mascarpone cheese
or crème fraîche
Butter for baking dish

Prepare the crêpes: Put the flour in a bowl, make a hole and add the eggs one at a time, mixing after each addition. Blend well, and then add the milk a little at a time, then the beer. Mix until the batter is smooth, then add the oil and salt.

Melt ½ teaspoon butter in a heavy skillet over medium-high heat. (Nonstick skillet works well.) Pour 3 tablespoons batter into the pan and lift off the heat source. Tip and swirl the pan to shape the batter into a 5–6 inch circle. Return to the heat and cook until bubbles form on the surface. Flip over for 5 seconds to brown lightly on the other side, then transfer to a plate. Continue in this manner until all the batter is used, coating the skillet with small amounts of butter every few crêpes, or as necessary.

Cook the frozen spinach, covered, in 1 tablespoon water for about 10 minutes. Drain and squeeze as much water as possible. In a bowl, mix the spinach, ricotta, eggs, half the Parmesan and nutmeg. Add salt and pepper, and set aside.

Prepare the coulis: Peel and chop the onion. Brown it in oil for 2 minutes, and add the tomatoes and concentrate, and ½ cup water, garlic (peeled and crushed) and thyme. Reduce, uncovered, over low heat for 15 minutes. Add salt and pepper to taste.

Preheat the oven to 400°F. In the center of each crêpe, put 2 level tablespoons of the filling, fold the sides and roll it.

Add the mascarpone to the tomato coulis. Arrange the rolled crêpes on a buttered baking dish, cover them with coulis, sprinkle the rest of the Parmesan, and bake for about 15 minutes. If you prepare this dish ahead of time, add the coulis at the last moment. This dish can also be served cold.

[tagliatelle with cabbage]

Remove the outer leaves and cut the cabbage in half. Cook it for 10 minutes in salted, boiling water: The cabbage should remain firm. Drain, discard the core and cut the leaves in fine strips.

Peel and chop the garlic. In a large skillet, brown it to a golden color in 3 tablespoons of the olive oil, then add the cabbage. Add salt, a generous amount of pepper and cook for 5 minutes, stirring. Add the mascarpone and set aside. Cut the ham in fine strips about ½ inch wide.

In a large pot of boiling water, with salt and a few drops of the oil, cook the noodles. When they are *al dente,* drain the noodles and put on a serving plate with the remaining oil. Toss well.

Reheat the cabbage for 1 minute, add the ham and pour over the noodles. Toss well and serve immediately with Parmesan cheese.

Serves 4-6
Prep time: 20 minutes
Cooking time: 15 minutes

½ head green cabbage
Salt
3 cloves garlic
6 tablespoons olive
  oil, divided
Pepper
9 ounces mascarpone
  cheese
6 ounces Parma ham
1 pound tagliatelle noodles
Freshly grated
  Parmesan cheese

[freshly made pasta]

On a work surface, mix the flour and the salt, and shape it into a mound. Make a well and break the eggs into it. Carefully keep blending the flour from the edges into the center of the thick dough, and knead it for 15 minutes until it is pliable and shiny. Wrap it in plastic wrap and let it rest for 1 hour.

Divide the dough in 4 parts. Flatten each one in thick sheets (¼ inch). Put them through the largest opening of the pasta machine. Flour each ribbon lightly, on both sides, and repeat the process 5 or 6 times, tightening the wheel each time. Dust the pasta with flour and leave it uncovered for 10 minutes, before cooking it.

Serves 6
Prep time: 30 minutes
Resting time: 1 hour
Cooking time: 4 minutes

1 pound sifted flour
½ teaspoon salt
5 eggs

[baked tagliatelle with prawns]

Serves 6
Prep time: 40 minutes
Cooking time:
about 30 minutes

2 pounds fresh or
  frozen prawns
Salt
2 white onions
2 cloves garlic
2 tablespoon olive oil
2 tablespoons butter
For the béchamel:
4 tablespoons butter
½ cup flour
1 cup milk
¼ cup dry white wine
Pepper
4 tablespoons crème fraîche
2 tablespoons Dijon
  mustard
1¼ pounds fresh or dried
  tagliatelle noodles
2 tablespoons chopped
  Italian parsley
2 ounces Parmesan cheese

Drop the langoustines in 1½ quarts of salted, boiling water and cook for 5 minutes. Take them out, but save the cooking water. Shell them and put the meat aside. Crush the shells and heads and put them back into the pot of water. Strain through a coffee filter and reserve 1¼ cups of the stock.

Peel the onions and cut them in thin slices. Peel and crush the garlic. Heat the oil and butter in a skillet and brown the onions for 5 minutes. Add the crushed garlic and remove from the heat.

Prepare the béchamel: Melt the butter, then add the flour and blend. Stirring constantly, add the reserved 1¼ cups stock, then the milk, the wine, and salt and pepper to taste. Add the sautéed onion and garlic, and cook over low hear just until the sauce coats a spoon. Remove from the heat, and add the crème fraîche, mustard and the langoustines, cut in small pieces.

Cook the tagliatelle in salted, boiling water for 6 minutes, until *al dente*.

Preheat the oven to 350°F. Drain the noodles and put them in a large oven dish, cover them with the béchamel and add the chopped parsley. Mix well. Sprinkle with Parmesan cheese and bake for about 10 minutes. Serve immediately.

Serves 6–8
Prep time: 30 minutes
Resting time: 15 minutes
Cooking time:
about 40 minutes

½ squash (17–18 inches
   in diameter)
Salt
4 eggs
2½ pounds flour
Butter
Grated Parmesan cheese

[pumpkin gnocchi]

Peel the pumpkin, remove the seeds and cut in big cubes. Cook for 30 minutes in salted, boiling water. Drain very well: You should have about 3 pounds of pulp.

Beat the warm pulp with a fork, adding the eggs one at a time. Gradually add the flour. When the dough becomes uniform and elastic, let it rest for 15 minutes. Butter a large platter and keep it warm in a 325°F oven.

Bring a large pot of salted water to a boil. Using 2 tablespoons dipped in the boiling water, scoop a ball of dough and drop it gently in the pot (if desired, each gnocchi may be shaped with the aid of a fork to give it ridges). Repeat the procedure for all the gnocchi. They are ready when they rise to the surface. Drain them and put them on the platter with a few pats of butter. Serve them with sage flavored butter (see page 40) and grated Parmesan cheese.

meat & fish

meat & fish

land and sea

Seafood is honored in Italy; perhaps because no place in that country is far from the magic of the sea and its culinary offerings. The fish of the Mediterranean are at their best in simple and enticing dishes. Veal is the preferred meat and, among fish, tuna is "the veal of the sea." Lamb is abundant in the South, whereas in the North of Italy, they raise beef and pork and produce tasty hams.

Serves 4–6
Prep time: 15 minutes
Cooking time: 10 minutes

Fresh or frozen gambas
  (large prawns; select
  3–4 per person)
Salt
For the pesto:
¼ cup fresh basil
¼ cup Italian parsley
2 ounces pine nuts
  or walnuts
2 cloves garlic
3 tablespoons
  Parmesan cheese
4 tablespoons olive oil
Pepper

[broiled gambas
with pesto]

Place the gambas on paper towels. With a sharp, pointed knife cut the gambas in two, lengthwise.

Put the split gambas, cut side up, on an oven tray covered with aluminum foil, and sprinkle with some salt.

Preheat the oven to 400°F. Place all the ingredients for the pesto in a food processor or blender and mix until well-blended. Spread it over the gambas.

Put the tray in the middle oven rack and cook the gambas for about 10 minutes.

[lamb in garlic cream]

Rinse the lamb shoulder and dry it with paper towels. Trim the fat with a sharp knife and make about a dozen slits on both sides of the meat. Mix the rosemary leaves with 1 teaspoon salt and 1 teaspoon pepper. Insert this aromatic mixture deeply into the slits. Put the meat in a roasting pan, drizzle with olive oil and sprinkle with any remaining aromatic mixture.

Separate the garlic cloves of one head, leaving the skin on, and distribute them around the meat. Cut the top from the second head of garlic, cover it with a few drops of oil, and a few rosemary leaves, and place on a sheet of aluminum foil. Enclose it in the foil and put it in the pan.

Pour ⅓ cup water in the roasting pan and put it in the oven (not pre-heated) to cook for 1 hour at 325°F, basting the meat often. Add the potatoes cut in thick wedges and cook for 30 minutes longer at 400°F. Five minutes before the end of the cooking time, remove the foil packet and let it cool. Press the garlic cloves with a fork and put the pulp in a small saucepan. Add the mascarpone and set the pan over low heat until it starts to boil. Remove from the heat, and add salt and pepper.

Put the meat, the potatoes and the roasted garlic cloves on a serving plate. Keep warm in the oven.

Deglaze the pan juices with 3 tablespoons water, scraping it well. Add this to the garlic cream and reheat it for 1 minute, and pour into a sauce pitcher. Serve warm.

Serves 6
Prep time: 15 minutes
Cooking time: 2 hours

1 choice lamb shoulder
8 branches fresh rosemary
Salt
Pepper
Olive oil
2 large heads garlic
12 medium-sized potatoes
1 cup mascarpone cheese

[veal with tuna]

Peel the garlic, onions and carrots. Cut the onions in quarters. Cut the celery and carrots in small pieces. Make small cuts into the roast and fill them with small pieces of garlic and anchovies. Put the roast in a stewing pan with the vegetables, the bouquet garni, the bouillon cube and the white wine. Cover the roast with water and bring the pot to a boil. Simmer it, covered, over medium heat, for 1 hour and 30 minutes. Reserve 2 tablespoons of the broth and let the meat cool.

Prepare the tuna sauce: Drain the tuna and the anchovies and mix them with a fork. Transfer to a bowl, add the egg yolk and some pepper. Whip the ingredients together, adding the olive oil a little at a time. Add the 2 tablespoons of the reserved broth, the lemon juice, crème fraîche and capers.

Cut the cold roast into thin slices. On a large platter, spread a thin layer of tuna sauce followed by the veal slices. With a spatula, evenly spread the remainder of the sauce over the veal slices. Cover it with plastic wrap and refrigerate overnight. Next day, decorate the edge of the platter with salad greens, cherry tomatoes, black olives and lemon wedges. This cold veal dish is ideal on a summer day.

Serves 6
Prep time: 30 minutes
Refrigeration time:
12 hours
Cooking time:
1 hour 30 minutes

4 cloves garlic
2 onions
2 carrots
3 ribs celery
3 pounds leg of veal,
  prepared for roasting
4 anchovy fillets in oil
1 bouquet garni
  (thyme, bay leaf
  and parsley)
1 bouillon cube
½ cup dry white wine

For the sauce:
1 can oil-packed tuna
  (6 ounces)
6 anchovies in oil
1 egg yolk
Pepper
⅓ cup olive oil
Juice of 1 lemon
2 tablespoons crème fraîche
2 tablespoons capers
  in vinegar
Salad greens
Cherry tomatoes
Black olives
Lemon wedges
  for decoration

[fish soup]

Serves 6
Prep time: 40 minutes
Cooking time:
1 hour 10 minutes

3 pounds fish (drum
  fish, sea bass, mullet,
  mackerel)
½ pound squid
For the stock:
2 shallots
2 tablespoons olive oil
1 pound tomato purée
2 fresh parsley branches
2 cloves garlic
2 small dry red peppers
Salt
2 leeks
2 fennel
2 pounds mussels
3 tablespoons olive oil
⅔ cup dry white wine
2 cloves garlic
1 teaspoon dried thyme
1 teaspoon dried oregano
1 teaspoon fennel seeds
¼ cup chopped basil, plus
  a few leaves for garnish
½ pound gambas
  (large prawns)
Pepper

Ask your fish vendor to fillet the fish, giving you the heads and back-bones, and ask the vendor to clean the squid.

Prepare the stock: Sauté the chopped shallots in olive oil. Add 6 cups of water, the tomato purée, parsley, chopped garlic, crushed peppers, the fish heads and bones and salt. Bring to a boil, cover the pot, and simmer for 30 minutes over low heat.

Wash and finely chop the leeks and fennel. Clean the mussels. Strain the stock, crushing the heads and bones. Cook the chopped leeks and fennel in the oil until soft, about 5 minutes over low heat. Pour in the wine and the stock, and add the chopped garlic, herbs, chopped basil and squid. Bring to a boil, covered, and let simmer for 30 minutes, stirring occasionally. Then add the fish, mussels and the prawns. Cover and let cook for 5–8 minutes— the fish should stay firm. Add salt and pepper, and serve the soup garnished with chopped basil.

[pesto]

Prep time: 5 minutes

1 small bunch fresh basil
1 small bunch fresh parsley
2 ounces pine nuts
  or walnuts
2 large cloves garlic
2 ounces Parmesan cheese
⅓ cup olive oil
Freshly ground pepper

Rinse and dry the basil. Process basil in a food processor or blender with the parsley, pine nuts, garlic and Parmesan. Gradually add the oil. The pesto must be smooth and firm. Add pepper to taste. This sauce should be prepared at the last minute.

To make sage pesto substitute 20 fresh sage leaves for the basil.

To make arugula pesto substitute 6 ounces of fresh chopped arugula leaves for the basil.

[polenta with herbs]

Rinse and dry the herbs and chop. In a large saucepan with a thick bottom, bring 6 cups of salted water to a boil. Pour the polenta slowly into the boiling water, whisking continuously (don't allow boiling to stop). Lower heat to a simmer and cook for about 30 minutes over low heat, stirring almost constantly with a wooden spoon, until the polenta leaves the sides of the pan. **R**emove from the heat, and add butter, herbs and pepper.* Spread the polenta about 1 inch thick on an oiled baking tray. When the polenta is set (takes about 1 hour), cut in squares, rounds or other desired shapes. Preheat the oven to 350°F. Drizzle the polenta pieces with olive oil, and add some salt and pepper. Place polenta in the oven for 20 minutes until golden brown.

*May be served at this point as soft polenta.

Serves 4–6
Prep time: 35 minutes
Resting time (if desired):
1 hour
Cooking time: 30 minutes

1 bunch Italian parsley
1 bunch fresh chives
2 teaspoons salt
1½ cups polenta
4 tablespoons butter
Pepper
¼ cup olive oil

[tuna preserved in oil]

Makes about 4 jars
Prep time: 25 minutes
Maceration time: 12 hours
Cooking time: 1 minute
Refrigeration time:
48 hours minimum

Salt
1 pound fresh tuna, sliced
1 lemon
6 cups fish or chicken
  broth (made with
  3 bouillon cubes)
Pepper
6 cloves garlic
Red and green pepper berries
4 bay leaves
4 branches fresh thyme
1¼ cups olive oil

Sprinkle salt on the tuna and rub it in well. Cover it. Wash and cut the lemon in ¼ inch slices, rub them with fine salt and cover.

Let the tuna and the lemon macerate for 12 hours in the refrigerator.

Next day, boil the broth for 5 minutes. Rinse the tuna in cool water, drop the pieces in the boiling court-bouillon and stop the heat when it picks up the boil. Cover and let cool.

Distribute the tuna, without skin or backbones, in the sterilized jars. Add a generous amount of pepper, the garlic cloves cut in half, the berries, bay leaves and thyme.

Rinse the lemon slices. Dry the slices well and add to the fish. Pour in the oil, close the jars tightly and keep refrigerated. The tuna will be ready 2 days later, and will keep for at least 3 weeks, refrigerated.

omodori pelati
Product of Italy

[saltimbocca]

With a meat mallet, pound the cutlets until they are thin and tender.

Put a piece of ham on top of each piece of veal and then a sage leaf. Fold each cutlet in two and hold it together with a wooden toothpick.

In a large skillet, brown the cutlets in half of the butter, over high heat, for 1 minute. Pour in the wine and let it reduce by half over high heat.

Remove the meat to a warm plate and salt and pepper it lightly. Mix the remaining butter with the meat juices in the pan, scraping the pan well. Pour sauce over the meat and serve immediately

Serves 4
Prep time: 15 minutes
Cooking time: 5 minutes

4 veal cutlets (scallops)
4 slices Parma ham
4 large fresh sage leaves
6 tablespoons butter,
   divided
⅓ cup dry white wine
Salt and pepper

[tomato sauce]

Plunge the tomatoes in boiling water for 1 minute. Let them cool and peel. Peel the onion and cut it in fine strips. Peel the garlic and put it through a garlic press.

Brown the onion and garlic in olive oil, for 2 minutes. Add the tomatoes, the concentrate, ½ cup water and a pinch of sugar. Add salt and pepper. Cover and simmer, over low heat, 45 minutes to 1 hour, stirring occasionally.

For fresh tomato sauce: Process the peeled tomatoes, add the garlic, onion, a little oregano or basil, and salt and pepper. Heat gently and keep warm while the pasta or gnocchi are cooking.

Any of the following can be added to the sauce: A small can of mashed anchovies in oil, 1 jar stuffed olives with anchovies, or ⅓ cup capers in vinegar and ½ cup pitted black olives.

Prep time: 10 minutes
Cooking time: about 1 hour

2 pounds fresh tomatoes,
   or 28 ounces canned
   crushed tomatoes
1 large sweet onion
2 cloves garlic
4 tablespoons olive oil
2 tablespoons tomato
   concentrate
Sugar
Salt and pepper

If you cannot find dried tomato paste, try preparing it with dried tomatoes in olive oil, using a blender.

[papillotes of trout with olives]

Peel and chop the shallots and garlic, and mix with the black olives and sage.

Remove the zest from the lemon and cut the fruit in half. Save the lemon for use later.

Coat each piece of fish with olive oil and put it on a square piece of oiled paper, or thick aluminum wrap. Next, spread a teaspoon of tomato purée over each one and add salt and pepper. Spread each one with the chopped olive mixture, followed by the capers and lemon zest. Sprinkle with lemon juice.

Fold the squares carefully, closing the ends, and place the papillotes on a baking sheet. Cook for 20 minutes in a preheated oven at 400°F.

Serves 4
Prep time: 15 minutes
Cooking time: 20 minutes

2 shallots
1 large clove garlic
12 pitted black olives
4 fresh sage leaves
Zest of 1 lemon, plus juice
4 trout fillets
  (6 ounces each)
Olive oil
4 teaspoons preserved
  dried tomatoes, puréed
Salt and pepper
1 tablespoon capers

[osso buco]

Serves 6
Prep time: 30 minutes
Cooking time: 2 hours–
2 hours 30 minutes

6 carrots
2 large onions
1 rib celery
3 pounds veal knuckles (6 rounds)
¼ cup flour
2 tablespoons butter
2 tablespoons olive oil
1 can crushed tomatoes (14 ounces)
¾ cup white wine
1 cube beef or chicken broth
2 tablespoon tomato concentrate
1 bouquet garni (parsley, thyme, bay leaf)
Salt and pepper
For the gremolada:
2 cloves garlic
A handful fresh parsley
2 sprigs fresh rosemary
6 fresh sage leaves
Zest of 1 lemon
Zest of ½ orange

Peel and mince the carrots and onions. Chop the celery in small pieces.

Coat the pieces of veal with flour. In a large pan, add the butter and olive oil, and brown the veal on both sides. Remove the meat and add the carrots, onion and celery. Cook for 2–3 minutes, on high heat, stirring constantly.

Put the meat back in the pan, and add the crushed tomatoes and cook, uncovered, for 10 minutes.

During this time, prepare a broth with ¾ cup water, the wine, bouillon cube and tomato concentrate. Bring to a boil.

Preheat the oven to 350°F.

Put the meat, vegetables and the bouquet garni in a cast iron pot with a cover. Add the broth, salt and pepper. Cover the pot and put it in the oven for 2 hours.

To prepare the gremolada: In a blender, mix the garlic, parsley, rosemary and sage. Add the zest of both fruits, finely cut. When the meat is ready, add the gremolada and serve.

A simple risotto made with 2 onions, 5 cups broth, ⅔ cup white wine and 2 cups Arborio rice is an excellent accompaniment for this dish.

[sardines au gratin]

Ask your fish vendor to filet the sardines. Put the fillets on a buttered au gratin dish, flesh side up. Plump the raisins in a bowl of warm water. Take about 3 handfuls of torn fresh bread, without the crust, convert them to crumbs in a food processor or blender, and fry them in the sunflower oil, until they are a light brown color. Zest 1 orange and add it to the crumbs along with the pine nuts and drained raisins. Mix well.

Preheat the oven to 350°F. Squeeze the zested orange and drizzle 3 tablespoon of the juice over the sardines. Coat sardines with 4 table-spoons of the olive oil, and some salt and pepper. Sprinkle the bread crumbs on top. Cook in the oven for 15 minutes.

Peel the 3 remaining oranges and slice them in rounds. Arrange them on a large plate, drizzle the remaining 2 tablespoons of olive oil over them and add some salt and pepper. Serve the warm sardines accompanied by the orange salad.

Serves 4
Prep time: 30 minutes
Cooking time: 15 minutes

2 pounds fresh sardines
1 tablespoon butter
¾ cup raisins
½ loaf fresh bread
¼ cup sunflower oil
4 oranges
2 ounces pine nuts
6 tablespoons olive
  oil, divided
Salt and pepper

[paupiettes of duck breast with fennel]

Peel the garlic and mince garlic, and add rosemary leaves, orange zest and fennel. Mix together and sprinkle with a generous amount of salt and pepper. Rub this aromatic mixture on the flesh of the duck breasts.

Bring together 2 pieces of meat on the flesh side. Hold each paupiette closed with wooden toothpicks, placing some toothpicks around the edges.

With a small, sharp knife, slash both sides several times.

Brown the paupiettes in the peanut oil for about 10 minutes. Cover and cook for 5 minutes over low heat. Remove the grease from the pan and add the wine. Simmer, partially covered, for 10–15 minutes (or until the duck is done according to taste).

Bring the paupiettes to the table, cut in half and surround with the sliced fennel.

Serves 6
Prep time: 15 minutes
Cooking time:
25–30 minutes

2 cloves garlic
30 sprigs fresh rosemary
  (about one 10 inch stem)
Zest of 1 orange
½ bouquet fennel
Salt and pepper
4 thick duck breasts
2 tablespoon peanut oil
½ cup "vino santo"
  or sherry
1 fresh fennel bulb,
  trimmed and sliced

To prepare the ratatouille: Chop 1 onion finely and sauté in 2 tablespoon of the olive oil. Chop the tomatoes and the seeded bell peppers, and add to the chopped onion together with the balsamic vinegar, sugar and Tabasco. Add salt to taste, cover and let simmer for 20 minutes, on low heat. Cut the polenta into even slices.

In the meantime, cook the polenta according to the package instructions. Cut the remaining onions in thin slices and brown in the remaining olive oil for 2 minutes. Preheat the oven to 425°F.

Spread the ratatouille on a large, rectangular baking pan. Cover with the sliced onions and then the slices of polenta. Distribute it evenly and sprinkle with grated Parmesan cheese. Top with a few pats of butter and brown in the oven for about 30 minutes. Serve the polenta cut in small squares.

Serves 4–6
Prep time: 30 minutes
Cooking time: 1 hour

3 onions
4 tablespoon olive oil, divided
1 can peeled tomatoes (14 ounces)
2 green bell peppers
2 red bell peppers
2 tablespoon balsamic vinegar
1 teaspoon powdered sugar
A few drops Tabasco sauce
Salt
1 tube precooked polenta
   (18 ounces; found in refrigerator section of market)
2 ounces Parmesan cheese
Butter

[polenta with ratatouille]

Not long ago, polenta was still a main dish among poor

peasants in northern Italy. This corn semolina, more or

less finely ground, was cooked for a long time in a

cauldron and nourished a whole family. Nowadays,

adopted by most countries, it is served with ragouts,

mainly rabbit, but also with vegetables. Cold and firm,

polenta cut in squares can be floured and fried in oil.

[cod with prune sauce]

Serves 4
Prep time: 15 minutes
Soaking time:
at least 24 hours
Cooking time: 1 hour

1¾ pounds salt cod
6 cups fish or chicken
  broth, made with
  3 bouillon cubes
Warm tomato sauce
  (see page 60)
25 large prunes
2 tablespoons chopped
  fresh parsley

Put the cod in a pan with cold water and let it desalt for about 24 hours, changing the water 3 or 4 times. Next day, bring the broth to a boil. Add the cod and when the broth returns to a boil remove from the heat, cover and let it cool.

Drain the cod and shred it, taking care to discard the skin and bones. Check the saltiness. If the fish is too salty, then put it in a pan with cold water and allow it to come to a boil. Drain the cod and rinse carefully in cold water.

Prepare the tomato sauce, according to the recipe given on page 60, but only cook the sauce (over low heat) for 30 minutes. Add the prunes and simmer for another 30 minutes, over low heat, adding a little water if the sauce seems too dry.

Add the pieces of cod to the sauce, and reheat for 2 minutes, without stirring. Serve sprinkled with parsley. Plain polenta is a good accompaniment.

[fried rabbit]

Serves 4
Prep time: 10 minutes
Cooking time: 30 minutes

1 rabbit cut in small
  pieces, with the bones
  (about 2½–3 pounds)
Flour
2 eggs
Salt and freshly
  ground pepper
Oil for frying
1 lemon cut in wedges

Thoroughly coat the pieces of rabbit with flour. Beat the eggs with salt and pepper. Heat about ½ inch of oil in a large skillet.

Quickly drop the rabbit pieces in the beaten egg. Fry them, over very low heat, for 5 minutes on each side. When they are brown, cover and simmer over low heat for 20 minutes, turning occasionally. Check the meat to make sure it's cooked by pricking a piece with a fork; the juice should be cream colored.

Drain on paper towels and serve, immediately, with lemon wedges and a mesclun salad (see page 92).

This cooking method is suitable for all meats, white or red. For boneless cuts such as chicken breasts, beef cutlets and veal scallops, cut in thin strips, cooking time is about 10 minutes.

[chicken casserole]

Serves 6
Prep time: 30 minutes
Cooking time:
1 hour 10 minutes

3 quarts chicken broth,
   made from 6 bouillon
   cubes
1 chicken
   (about 3½ pounds)
1 leek
2 carrots
2 ribs celery
1 small red or yellow
   bell pepper
3 tablespoon olive oil
For the crisp crust:
⅓ cup flour
2 ounces Parmesan cheese
2 tablespoons
   bread crumbs
4 tablespoons cold butter,
   in small pieces
Salt and freshly
   ground pepper

In a large pot, bring the broth to a boil and add the whole chicken. Cover and let simmer for 1 hour. In the meantime, prepare the vegetables: Wash and peel the leek, carrots and celery, and cut in small pieces. Wash and seed the bell pepper and cut in small pieces. In a large skillet, brown the vegetables in olive oil for 15 minutes, stirring often.

Prepare the crust: Mix the flour, Parmesan, bread crumbs and pieces of butter with your fingertips until it resembles coarse meal. Preheat the oven to 400°F.

Drain the chicken and reserve 1¼ cups of broth. Remove the skin and bones, and cut the meat in small pieces. Distribute the meat on a buttered baking pan, cover it with the vegetables, moisten with the cooking broth, and add salt and pepper. Sprinkle the crust mixture on top and place in the oven for 10–15 minutes until the top is crisp. Serve the casserole with a small salad (see page 92).

vegetables—
hot and cold,
crunchy or soft

Italian cooking, like all Mediterranean cuisine, uses vegetables without relegating them to the role of accompaniments. Always chosen very fresh and tender, they are often flavored and served with olive oil. As a rule, they are cooked longer than vegetables in most modern cuisine, and should be soft.

Serves 6
Prep time: 20 minutes
Cooking time: 5–7 minutes

½ cauliflower
3 carrots
4 endives
1 stalk celery
2 fennel bulbs
2 red bell peppers
1 cucumber
3 tomatoes
1 bunch red radishes
For the sauce:
7–8 cloves garlic
4 ounces anchovies in oil
8 tablespoons butter
  (1 stick)
½ cup olive oil
½ cup crème fraîche

[bagna cauda]

Peel, wash and cut all the vegetables in sticks, pieces or divide them in flowerettes. Arrange on a large plate.

To prepare the sauce: Peel the garlic and chop the garlic and the anchovies. In a fondue pot, or chafing dish, melt the butter and add the garlic with the anchovies. Stir the mixture until it is soft, and then add the olive oil, a little at a time, stirring continuously. Do not let it boil.

When it gets hot, add the crème fraîche and simmer, over low heat, for 5 minutes to thicken it.

Put the fondue pot with its warmer in the center of the table. Each guest will dip the crudités of his choice into the sauce.

[minestrone]

Serves 6–8
Prep time: 30 minutes
Cooking time: 1 hour

2 carrots
½ pound potatoes
2 stalks celery
2 zucchini
2 onions
3 cloves garlic
¼ green cabbage
½ pound fresh peas
¼ pound smoked bacon
6 tablespoon olive oil,
  divided
1 small can chopped
  tomatoes (15 ounces)
3 tablespoons tomato paste
1 sugar cube
5 tablespoon chopped
  fresh basil, divided
1 sprig fresh thyme
Salt and freshly
  ground pepper
1 small can white beans
4 ounces small size pasta
Freshly grated Parmesan
  to garnish
Pesto to garnish

Wash and peel the carrots and the potatoes then dice. Wash and dice the celery and the zucchini. Peel and chop the onions and garlic. Cut the cabbage in thin strips and shell the green peas. Cut the smoked bacon in small cubes.

In a large pot, brown the bacon and onions in 3 tablespoons of the olive oil. After they begin to brown, add the carrots, the celery and 1 garlic clove. Cook for 5 minutes.

Add the tomatoes with their juice, the tomato paste, the sugar, 2 tablespoons of the basil, the thyme, 2 quarts of water and some salt and pepper. Cover and simmer for 20 minutes, stirring occasionally. Add the potatoes and the zucchini, cover, and cook for 10 minutes. Add the green peas and cabbage, and cook for 15 minutes more, covered. Finally, add the white beans and the pasta. Cook, uncovered, for 10 minutes. At the end of the cooking, add the rest of the olive oil, basil and chopped garlic and check the seasoning. If the soup tends to stick to the sides, add some water, however, it should be rather thick.

Serve in a soup tureen, sprinkled with Parmesan. Place more cheese and a bowl of pesto (see page 57) on the table.

[eggplant au gratin]

Wash and cut off the ends of the eggplant. Cut them, lengthwise, in slices about ½ inch thick. Salt and let them drain for 1 hour. In the meantime, boil the tomatoes a few seconds, peel them, remove the seeds and chop them. In a saucepan, lightly brown the chopped garlic and basil in olive oil, for 1 minute. Add the tomatoes, salt and pepper to taste and cook for 30 minutes.

In a large skillet, heat the frying oil. Rinse the eggplant slices in fresh water, dry them, flour lightly, and fry for 2 minutes on each side. When they are done, set them on paper towels. Slice the mozzarella cheese.

Preheat the oven to 350°F. Butter a baking dish and put a layer of eggplant on the bottom, then add some tomato sauce, cover with a layer of mozzarella slices and sprinkle with Parmesan cheese. Continue this layering, ending with mozzarella on top. Sprinkle with Parmesan cheese and bake in the oven for 35 minutes.

This gratin is the perfect accompaniment for grilled meat or baked fish.

Serves 6
Prep time: 20 minutes
Resting time: 1 hour
Cooking time: 35 minutes

4 large eggplants
Salt
1¾ pounds tomatoes
2 cloves garlic
3 tablespoons fresh basil
4 tablespoons olive oil
Pepper
Oil for frying
6 tablespoons flour
6 ounces mozzarella
1 tablespoon butter
Freshly grated
  Parmesan cheese

[zucchini soup]

Serves 6–8
Prep time: 10 minutes
Cooking time: 35 minutes

2 pounds zucchini
1 onion
4 tablespoons butter
2 chicken or vegetable
  bouillon cubes
Salt
2 eggs
3 tablespoons
  Parmesan cheese
3 tablespoons chopped
  fresh basil, divided
Pepper

Wash, cut off the ends and slice the zucchini in ½-inch-thick rounds. Peel and mince the onion. In a large pot, brown the onion in butter. Add the zucchini and sauté for about 10 minutes, stirring occasionally.

Prepare broth by dissolving the bouillon cubes in 2 quarts of water. Pour the boiling broth over the zucchini. Add salt, cover, and simmer for 20 minutes on low heat. Purée in a food processor or blender.

In a soup tureen, beat the eggs with the Parmesan and 1 tablespoon of the chopped basil. Pour in the hot soup, a little at a time, beating continuously. Add salt and pepper and the rest of the basil. Serve immediately with additional Parmesan cheese.

This soup can be reheated the next day, but do not boil the soup.

[coulis of red peppers]

Serves 6
Prep time: 15 minutes
Cooking time: 35 minutes

1¾ pounds red bell peppers
2 medium-sized tomatoes
3 onions
1 clove garlic
2 tablespoons olive oil
Salt and pepper
5 ounces crème fraîche

Wash the bell pepper, and remove the ends and the seeds. Cut the bell pepper in small pieces.

Boil the tomatoes for a few seconds, cool and peel. Discard the seeds. Chop tomatoes and add to the bell peppers.

Peel and mince the onions and garlic, and sauté in a large skillet for 2 minutes in olive oil, over low heat. Add the bell peppers and the tomatoes, and salt and pepper to taste. Pour in ¼ cup water, cover, and let simmer for 30 minutes.

Let cool completely before puréeing in a food processor or blender, then add the crème fraîche, blend and serve.

[mashed potatoes
with olive oil]

Peel, wash and quarter the potatoes. Drop in 2 quarts of salted, boiling water and cook for 20 minutes, after they start boiling. Drain. Boil the milk with the nutmeg and bay leaf.

Put the warm potatoes through a potato press. Stir them gently while slowly adding the olive oil, then the hot milk (without the bay leaf). Toss gently and add the mascarpone, and Parmesan, and season with salt and pepper.

Serves 4
Prep time: 15 minutes
Cooking time: 25 minutes

3½ pounds baking potatoes
Salt
1¼ cups milk
1 pinch freshly grated nutmeg
1 bay leaf
¼ cup olive oil
3 tablespoons
   mascarpone cheese
2 ounces Parmesan cheese
Salt and pepper

Serves 6
Prep time: 15 minutes
Cooking time: 10 minutes

2 pounds fresh or
  frozen fava beans
Salt
6 ounces fresh
  baby spinach
6 tablespoon crème fraîche
Juice of 1 lemon
6 tablespoon olive oil
Pepper
½ cup pitted black olives
  (3–4 ounces)
A few fresh mint leaves
Small mint or basil leaves
  to garnish (optional)

[fresh fava beans
with spinach]

Drop the fava beans in a pan of salted, boiling water and cook for 10 minutes, after they pick up the boil.

Separate and wash the spinach and squeeze the water out. In a big bowl, mix the crème fraîche, lemon juice, olive oil, salt and pepper, to make the dressing.

Drain the fava beans. If they are young, leave their skin on, otherwise, remove the skins by pressing the beans with 2 fingers.

Put the warm fava beans in the bowl. Add the raw spinach and the olives, toss gently with the dressing and sprinkle with the chopped mint. Garnish with mint or basil leaves if you're using.

[tagliatelle of zucchini with anise]

Serves 4
Prep time: 15 minutes
Cooking time: 5 minutes

4 large firm zucchini
Juice of 1 lemon
2 tablespoon pastis
  or pernod
2 teaspoons anise seed
2 teaspoons chopped
  fresh chives
6 tablespoons olive oil
Salt and pepper

Wash and cut off the ends of the zucchini. Using a sharp knife, cut lengthwise into thin slices, then cut lengthwise downward into slices to resemble the long, thin flat strips of tagliatelle. Sprinkle with the juice of ½ of the lemon.

Steam the zucchini for 5 minutes. It should remain crisp.

In a bowl, mix the remaining lemon juice, the pastis, anise seed and chives. Add the olive oil, and salt and pepper to taste.

Put the drained zucchini, still warm, on a plate, and pour the sauce over the zucchini. Toss and serve.

[warm beans in vinaigrette]

Serves 6
Prep time: 10 minutes
Cooking time: 1 hour
30 minutes–2 hours
Soaking time: 1–2 hours

1 pound large dried
  white beans
¼ cup olive oil
For the vinaigrette:
4 anchovy fillets in oil
2 cloves garlic
1 small bunch fresh parsley
Juice of 2 lemons
¼ cup olive oil
Salt and pepper
2 sweet white onions

Wash the beans, and place them in a saucepan with 6 cups of water. Bring to a boil and boil for 2 minutes. Cover and let them soak for 1–2 hours.

Bring the beans back to a boil. Cover and cook, over low heat, for 1 hour and 30 minutes to 2 hours: The beans should be tender but not split.

Drain them and place in a bowl with the olive oil. Keep covered.

In a blender, mix the anchovies, garlic and parsley leaves until well combined. Add the lemon juice and then the olive oil, slowly, with the blender continuously running. Add salt and pepper.

Peel and thinly slice the onions. Pour the vinaigrette over the beans, toss and scatter the onion rings on top. Serve the dish warm.

The following recipe is intended for green asparagus. However, if you can find wild asparagus use them—omitting the steam cooking if they are very thin.

[asparagus sautéed with thyme and olives]

Steam cook the asparagus for 5 minutes. In a large pan, sauté asparagus in the olive oil and thyme leaves, turning carefully.

As soon as the asparagus begin to brown, add the olives and cook for 1 minute longer. Add salt and pepper and serve immediately. Garnish with cherry tomatoes, if desired.

Asparagus can be a tasty accompaniment to grilled fish, fried rabbit or fried meat.

Serves 4
Prep time: 15 minutes
Cooking time: 7 minutes

2 pounds fresh or frozen
  green asparagus
¼ cup olive oil
4 sprigs fresh thyme
8 ounces pitted green
  olives, sliced or whole
Salt and pepper
Cherry tomatoes for
  garnish (optional)

[mushroom terrine]

Serves 6–8
Prep time: 25 minutes
Cooking time: 2 hours

3½ pounds potatoes
1 pound onions
8 tablespoons olive oil, divided
4 large cloves garlic
1 bunch fresh parsley
1½ pounds mushrooms
Salt and pepper

For the vinaigrette:
2 tablespoons
balsamic vinegar
2 tablespoons dried
tomato purée
¼ cup olive oil
Salt and pepper

Peel and cut the potatoes in thin slices, if possible using a food processor or mandoline. Peel and mince the onions and brown in a skillet with 3 tablespoons of the olive oil.

Peel and chop the garlic. Chop the parsley. Clean the mushrooms, wash them quickly in cold water and slice thinly.

In an oiled terrine, put half of the potatoes and sprinkle with salt and pepper, followed by half each of the onion, garlic and parsley. Next, add half of the mushrooms. Then put on the other half of the onions, mushrooms, garlic and parsley, and finish with the other half of the potatoes. Add salt and pepper. Drizzle with the remaining olive oil. Cover the terrine with its top or with foil, and cook for 2 hours in a preheated 325°F oven.

Mix the vinegar and the purée of dried tomatoes. Slowly add the olive oil, stirring constantly. Add salt and pepper to taste. Serve the terrine, warm or cold, with the vinaigrette on the side.

[confits of fennel and onions]

Preheat the oven to 350°F. Peel the onions and cut 8 of them in half, horizontally, and thinly slice the last one. Arrange the halved onions on a pan coated with olive oil, and add salt and pepper. Put them in the oven and cook for 15 minutes. Pour half of the vinegar over the onions and cook for another 15 minutes. Pour the rest of the vinegar, turn off the oven and leave the onions in the oven to keep warm.

Wash the fennel and cut them in half or quarters (depending on their thickness), after cutting off the top of the stalks. Flour them and brown in olive oil in a large skillet, with the sliced onion, for 5 minutes. Pour in the white wine, scraping the pan to loosen the drippings. Add ½ cup water, the thyme, rosemary and bay leaves. Add salt and pepper. Simmer for 15 minutes, stirring occasionally.

Arrange the onions and the fennel on a large plate and sprinkle with the chopped basil. The confits can be enjoyed hot or cold, with grilled fish.

Serves 4
Prep time: 20 minutes
Cooking time: 1 hour

9 medium-sized
  white onions
Olive oil to coat pan
Salt and pepper
8 tablespoons balsamic
  vinegar, divided
4–8 fennel (depending
  on their thickness)
4 tablespoons flour
4 tablespoons olive oil
¼ cup white wine
1 sprig fresh thyme
1 sprig fresh rosemary
2 bay leaves
A few fresh basil leaves

[flan with tomato coulis]

Preheat the oven to 350°F and prepare a bain-marie*. Beat the eggs, and add the crème fraîche and then the tomato coulis. Add salt and pepper. Rinse and dry the chives, mince them and add them to the eggs.

Pour the mixture in a soufflé dish or a charlotte mold, and cook for 50 minutes in the bain-marie. If the flan is browning too fast, cover it with aluminum foil while it is cooking. Serve it hot, warm or cold, as you prefer.

*To prepare a bain-marie, fill a pan large enough to hold the soufflé (for the flan) with enough hot water to reach about halfway up the sides of the soufflé dish. Set the flan-filled soufflé dish in the pan of hot water.

Serves 6
Prep time: 10 minutes
Cooking time: 50 minutes

6 eggs
⅔ cup crème fraîche
1 pound tomato coulis
  or purée
Salt and pepper
½ bunch fresh chives

Remove the brown part of the stems and wash the mushrooms quickly. Dry the mushrooms well and cut in half or quarters. Place in a large pot with the coarse salt and cook for about 10 minutes over medium heat. Discard the liquid several times. When the mushrooms do not give out any more liquid, add the vinegar and 1¼ cups water and bring to a boil. Transfer the mushrooms to a colander and drain for about 30 minutes.

Distribute the mushrooms, bay leaves and peppercorns in the jars, previously sterilized. Cover with olive oil and close the jars. Keep the jars in a cool, dry place until needed. The fragrant oil can also be used.

Makes about 3 jars
(about 1¼ cups each)
Prep time: 20 minutes
Liquid reduction time:
30 minutes
Cooking time: 10 minutes

2 pounds fresh mushrooms
3 tablespoons coarse salt
1¼ cups white vinegar
3 bay leaves
15 peppercorns
1¼ cups olive oil

[mushrooms in oil]

Italians love mushrooms and will cross borders to gather their favorite variety. They have a treasure in the famous and expensive white truffle from Albe, and the black truffle of Umbria. They also enjoy "cepes," called porcini (little pigs), morels and many more—so rare and delicious...

[little salads]

Mesclun: Wash and sort the salad greens. Wash, and dry the chervil and pull off the leaves. Prepare the vinaigrette by mixing all the ingredients. Pour the dressing over the salad just before serving it.

In the same manner, you can prepare a salad with baby spinach. Use 12 ounces spinach. Wash and dry the leaves, toss with a few radicchio leaves and cover the salad with vinaigrette.

Sautéed radicchio: Wash and dry the radicchio and quarter, lengthwise. Rinse, dry and chop the parsley. Cook the radicchio for 1 minute, in olive oil. Sprinkle the parsley and salt and pepper over the radicchio, and sauté for 1 more minute. Serve hot or cold with fish or meat.

Sautéed dandelions: Clean the dandelions and drop them in 1 quart of salted, boiling water, and cook for 1 minute. Drain well and cut them about 2½ inches long. Peel and chop the shallots. Cook dandelions and shallots in a skillet in the olive oil, for 2 minutes. Add salt and pepper to taste.

Mesclun
Serves 4
Prep time: 5 minutes

4 ounces arugula (rocket)
4 ounces purslane
  or watercress
A few sprigs fresh chervil
For the vinaigrette:
Juice of 1 lemon
6 tablespoon olive oil
Salt and pepper

Sautéed radicchio
Serves 4
Prep time: 5 minutes
Cooking time: 2 minutes

4–8 radicchio,
  depending on size
1 bunch Italian parsley
6 tablespoons olive oil
Salt and pepper

Sautéed dandelions
Serves 4
Prep time: 5 minutes
Cooking time: 5 minutes

2 pounds dandelions
Salt
2 shallots
6 tablespoons olive oil
Pepper

Serves 6
Prep time: 15 minutes
Cooking time: 30 minutes

5 medium-sized potatoes
2 carrots
1 onion
1 rib celery
8 yellow bell peppers
5 tablespoons olive
    oil, divided
⅓ cup milk
Salt and pepper
2 ounces grated
    Parmesan cheese
A few garlic croutons

[cream of yellow pepper soup]

Peel the potatoes, carrots and onion. Wash the celery and the bell peppers and remove the seeds from the bell peppers. Finely chop the onion, carrots and celery, and sauté for 5 minutes in a large pot with 3 tablespoons of the olive oil. When they are golden brown, add the bell peppers cut in small pieces and the potatoes cut in cubes. Pour in the milk, and enough water so that the liquid covers the vegetables. Salt and pepper to taste and simmer, covered, for 20 minutes. When the potatoes are very tender, process the soup in a blender or food processor. Serve the soup hot, in a tureen, with a drizzle of olive oil. Sprinkle with the Parmesan. Accompany with the garlic croutons.

desserts

desserts

sweet and sour

The sweets of the Italian Peninsula are somewhat extravagant. Is it the profusion of candied fruits, the abundant use of vanilla, or the ever-present whipped cream? The secret is to select the best and simplest ingredients, and combine them with sugar, a touch of spices and bitter flavors. Often the zest of citrus fruits, rosemary, coffee, cocoa beans and bitter almond (as in macaroons called, amaretti) give Italian desserts their unique flavor.

Serves 4
Prep time: 15 minutes

1 large melon
Powdered sugar
2 cups mixed seasonal
  berries, divided
1 teaspoon vanilla
6 tablespoons
  balsamic vinegar

[melon carpaccio with red berry coulis]

Peel the melon, cut it in half and discard the seeds. Using a big knife with a flat blade, cut thin slices and arrange attractively on a large plate. Sprinkle with some powdered sugar.

In a blender, prepare the red berry coulis by mixing one cup of the berries with a bit of powdered sugar (depending on the sweetness of the berries), vanilla and balsamic vinegar.

When ready to serve, arrange the remaining berries over the carpaccio and offer the berry coulis on the side.

[pears with mascarpone in papillote]

Serves 4
Prep time: 15 minutes
Cooking time: 25 minutes

4 ripe firm pears
4 ounces mascarpone
  cheese
2 teaspoons honey
4 tablespoons sugar
1 tablespoon
  ground cinnamon

Peel the pears, keeping the stems on. Cut them in half and core. Mix the mascarpone and honey. Fill the hollows of the pears with the mascarpone-honey and put each pear halve back together with two wooden toothpicks.

Mix the sugar and cinnamon and roll the pears in the sugar-cinnamon mixture to coat.

Preheat the oven to 350°F. Place each fruit in the middle of a large rectangle of baking paper. Enclose the pears in the paper, folding to make an airtight packet, and put them close together on a baking tray. Place on the middle oven rack and bake for 25 minutes.

Serve each papillote, partly open, on a dessert plate.

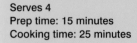

[macaroon tart]

Coarsely grind the hazelnuts and almonds, then mix them with the sugar and flour.

Beat the egg whites with the salt until stiff. Fold them carefully into the nuts. Preheat the oven to 350°F.

Generously butter a 15-inch-diameter tart pan. Add the batter and bake for 20–30 minutes. Let it cool and unmold the tart.

You can enjoy this tart, warm or cold, with a crème anglaise made with the unused yolks.

Serves 6
Prep time: 10 minutes
Cooking time:
20–30 minutes

4 ounces shelled
  whole hazelnuts
4 ounces shelled
  whole almonds
1⅔ cups powdered sugar
1 tablespoon flour
3 egg whites
Pinch salt
Butter for tart pan

[semi-freddo]

Serves 4–6
Prep time: 45 minutes
Cooking time: 35 minutes
Freezing time: 30 minutes

4 apples
5 tablespoons white wine
1⅓ cups powdered
  sugar, divided
Grated zest of 1 lemon
4 egg yolks
½ cup crème fraîche
5 ounces amaretti or
  almond macaroons

1 layer cake or pound cake

Peel the apples, cut in thin slices and simmer in a saucepan with 3 tablespoons water, the wine, ¼ cup of the sugar and the lemon zest for 10 minutes. Beat the egg yolks and the remaining sugar in a small bowl. Place the bowl over a saucepan with barely simmering water (don't allow water to touch the bottom of the bowl).

Beat constantly until mixture registers 140°F. Continue beating over simmering water for 3 minutes and then remove bowl from water. Using electric mixer beat until cool and thick, about 5 minutes. Beat the crème fraîche using an electric mixer until peaks form. Add the egg mixture and gently fold together. Fold in puréed apples and crushed amaretti.

Line a loaf pan with plastic wrap. Slice cake horizontally in 3 pieces. Put bottom cake layer in bottom of loaf pan. Spread on ½ of creme mixture and top with middle layer of cake. Spread on the remaining creme and top with last layer of cake. Cover with plastic wrap and freeze for at least 8 hours. At serving time, remove the plastic wrap and invert the loaf pan on a platter. Peel off the rest of the plastic wrap. Cut in 1-inch-thick slices and serve. Keep any remaining cake in the freezer.

[ricotta tart]

Serves 6
Prep time: 20 minutes
Resting time: 1 hour
Cooking time: 45 minutes

For the pastry:
1¾ cups flour
6 tablespoons
  granulated sugar
1 pinch salt
7 tablespoons
  softened butter
Zest of 1 lemon
1 egg, plus 1 yolk
12 ounces ricotta
3 ounces crème fraîche
6 tablespoons
  granulated sugar
3 eggs
Grated zest of 1 orange
2 tablespoon raisins
2 ounces candied fruits
2 tablespoons
  slivered almonds
Butter for tart mold

To prepare the pastry: Make a well in the flour and add the sugar, salt, butter, lemon zest and whole egg, plus the yolk. Work the dough with your fingers until it forms a solid ball (if it breaks apart, add 1 tablespoon of cold water). Cover it with a cloth and let it rest for 1 hour.

Preheat the oven to 400°F. Mix the ricotta, crème fraîche and sugar in a bowl. Add the eggs, orange zest, raisins, candied fruits chopped in little pieces and the slivered almonds. Mix well.

Roll the pastry dough until it is very thin. Place in a buttered tart mold (15 inches in diameter). Fill it with the fruit mixture and bake in the oven for 45 minutes. Serve the tart warm or cold.

[chilled apple mousse]

Serves 6
Prep time: 25 minutes
Refrigeration time:
at least 1 hour
Cooking time: 40 minutes

5 large apples
1 teaspoon vanilla
⅓ cup sugar
Pinch ground cinnamon
⅔ cup milk
2 eggs, plus 2 yolks
Butter for cake pan

Peel and slice the apples. Cook in 2 tablespoons water with the vanilla, sugar and cinnamon, over low heat for 20 minutes.

Boil the milk. Beat the eggs and egg yolks lightly, add the hot apple mixture to the eggs and whisk vigorously. Pour in the hot milk, stirring continuously.

Pour into a buttered cake pan. Preheat the oven to 350°F and prepare a bain-marie (see page 88). Put the mold in the bain-marie and bake in the oven for 40 minutes. Let it cool before refrigerating it for 1 hour.

Remove the mold from the dessert and serve surrounded with a coulis of red fruits (see page 97).

[french toast from panettone]

Cut the panettone in thick slices. In a bowl, beat the eggs with the vanilla, sugar and milk, beating well. Pour the mixture into a shallow dish.

Heat 1$^1/_2$ tablespoons of the butter in a frying pan set over low heat. Dip each slice of panettone in the eggs and brown for 2 minutes on each side, adding butter as needed.

Put the slices on a plate and sprinkle with sugar when ready to serve.

Serves 6–8
Prep time: 5 minutes
Cooking time:
about 5 minutes

1 panettone
4 eggs
1 teaspoon vanilla
2 teaspoons sugar
1¼ cups milk
6 tablespoons
   butter, divided
Sugar

Serves 6
Prep time: 15 minutes
Freezing time: 3 hours

3 lemons
1½ cups sugar
A few fresh mint leaves

[lemon ice]

Brush the lemons under warm water. Zest 2 of the lemons. Squeeze the juice from all the lemons.

Bring 1¼ cups water, the sugar and the zest to a boil. Cook for 3 minutes until the sugar is completely dissolved. Add the lemon juice and let it cool completely.

Pour the syrup in freezer trays and put in the freezer for 1 hour.

Remove and stir well to mix the crystals with the liquid. Repeat this procedure every 30 minutes, or 5 times during the freezing period.

Serve in goblets decorated with chopped mint leaves, lemon zest or colorful candies, as desired.

[apple tart with rosemary]

Preheat the oven to 400°F. Unroll the dough and fit it in a 1-inch tart mold.

Pull the leaves off the rosemary. Peel and cut the apples in thin slices and distribute over the pastry dough, packing them well. Sprinkle with sugar and top with half of the butter, cut in small pieces.

Bake it in the oven for 20 minutes. Sprinkle with rosemary and the remaining butter, cut in pieces. Bake for 10 minutes more and serve warm or cold.

Serves 6
Prep time: 15 minutes
Cooking time: 30 minutes

1 readymade pie crust
5 fresh rosemary sprigs
6 apples
1 cup powdered sugar
8 tablespoons butter
 (1 stick)

[sabayon]

Beat the egg yolks with the sugar over a bain-marie (see page 88). Add the Marsala, a little at a time, until the mixture is thick and creamy (this will take 5–10 minutes). The sabayon must not boil, only thicken.

Serve it warm or cold, perhaps with fruits poached in wine and spices.

You could also top the sabayon with red fruits or other fruits in season, and put under the broiler for 2 minutes.

For a chilled sabayon, prepare in the same manner. After it is removed from the heat, add the grated zest of 1 lemon and let it cool.

Whisk ¾ cup crème fraîche and then add it carefully to the cool sabayon. Pour it into individual bowls and place in the refrigerator for at least 2 hours.

Serve the chilled sabayon by itself, or on a plate decorated with strawberry coulis, red fruits or fruit poached in wine.

Serves 4–6
Prep time: 10 minutes
Cooking time:
5–10 minutes

6 egg yolks
⅔ cup sugar
1½ tablespoons dry
 Marsala or port

If you like the slight bitterness of cappuccino, a pleasant coffee drink known all over the world, you will adore this simple and delicate dessert. Nothing prevents you from adding a sprinkle of bitter cocoa...

[cream of cappuccino]

Heat the milk with the instant coffee. Beat the egg yolks and the whole egg with the sugar until they look white. Pour the hot milk over the eggs, while constantly whisking the mixture.

Preheat the oven to 350°F and prepare a bain-marie (see page 88).

Fill small ramekins or ovenproof coffee cups with the cream of cappuccino and set them in the bain-marie (see page 88). Put them in the oven to bake for 30 minutes. Let them cool before chilling for a minimum of 1 hour.

When ready to serve, decorate with whipped cream and sprinkle powdered dark chocolate over the top.

Serves 4
Prep time: 10 minutes
Cooking time: 30 minutes
Refrigeration time:
at least 1 hour

1¼ cups whole milk
4 teaspoons instant coffee
3 egg yolks, plus
  1 whole egg
⅔ cup powdered sugar
Whipped cream
Powdered dark chocolate
  for decoration

[baked stuffed peaches]

Serves 4
Prep time: 20 minutes
Cooking time: 30 minutes

5 large peaches
Butter for baking dish
3 macaroons
1 egg yolk
1 teaspoon vanilla
2 ounces shelled almonds, coarsely ground
Grated zest of ½ lemon
Slivered almonds
¼ cup vino santo or sherry
1 tablespoon sugar
Whole almonds and poppy seeds (optional)

Cut the peaches in half and remove the pits. Put 8 halves on a buttered, baking dish with the cut side up. Peel the two other halves; and set them aside.

In a food processor, mix the macaroons, the egg yolk, vanilla and the flesh of the 5th peach. Blend the coarsely ground almonds with the mixture; then add the lemon zest.

Preheat the oven to 325°F.

Distribute the filling in the peach cavities and place a few slivered almonds on top. Pour the wine over the peaches and sprinkle with the sugar. Bake for 30 minutes.

Serve the peaches warm, or at room temperature, garnished with whole almonds and sprinkled with poppy seeds, if desired.

[chocolate mousse]

Serves 6
Prep time: 15 minutes
Cooking time: 30 minutes

6 tablespoons butter
5 ounces semisweet
  chocolate
6 medium eggs
½ cup sugar
4 tablespoons cornstarch
Pinch salt
Butter for cake pan

In a bain-marie (see page 88), melt the butter with the chocolate, broken in pieces. When the mixture is uniform, remove from the heat.

Break the eggs, separating the whites from the yolks. In a bowl, mix the sugar with the cornstarch. One by one, add the egg yolks until they turn almost white. Next, add the melted chocolate and mix well.

Preheat the oven to 350°F. Beat the egg whites with a pinch of salt. With a fork, fold them carefully into the chocolate mixture. Transfer to a buttered cake pan and bake it in the oven for 30 minutes.

[chestnut cake]

Melt the butter and allow it to cool a bit.
Break the eggs, separating the whites from the yolks. In a bowl, beat the yolks, melted butter, vanilla and powdered sugar until the mixture is almost white. Add the chestnut purée and the powdered hazelnuts. Mix well.

Preheat the oven to 350°F. Beat the egg whites with a pinch of salt and fold them carefully into the batter. Transfer into a buttered cake pan and bake for 35 minutes, or until the cake springs back when touched in the center.

You can enjoy this cake warm or cold. It will almost be better the following day. You could also add 1 tablespoon rum to the batter, according to taste.

Serves 6
Prep time: 10 minutes
Cooking time: 35 minutes

7 tablespoons butter
3 eggs
1 teaspoon vanilla
1½ cups powdered sugar
⅔ cup unsweetened
  chestnut purée (7 ounces)
5 ounces hazelnuts,
  ground to a powder
Pinch salt
Butter for cake pan

ZANETTI

Andorra Express
MADE IN ITALY

Wash the peaches and cut them in half. Remove the pit. In an attractive serving bowl, place the peaches cut side up.
Pour wine into the bowl until the peaches float. Cover and chill for 1 hour.
Serve the sparkling peaches, cold, decorated with a few mint leaves.

Serves 6
Prep time: 5 minutes
Refrigeration time: 1 hour

6 large ripe peaches
2 cups cool sparkling wine
A few fresh mint leaves

[sparkling peaches]

Tiramisu (literally means "pick-me-up") is, undoubtedly,

the best known Italian dessert. It was created, or rather

recreated, from a traditional recipe in Sienna called

"zuppa inglese." It has recently been revised by changing

the sabayon to a cream of mascarpone. The amaretto can

be replaced by a bitter almond Marsala.

[tiramisu]

Beat the egg yolks with the powdered sugar until they look white. Add the mascarpone, beating with a mixer, on low speed for 1 minute.

In a separate bowl, beat the chilled crème fraîche until firm. With a fork, add it carefully to the mascarpone. In a shallow dish, mix the coffee with the amaretto, if using.

Line the bottom of a bowl (12 inches in diameter) with ladyfingers dipped quickly in the coffee-amaretto (or just coffee), layer half of the cream over the ladyfingers, add another layer of dipped ladyfingers and cover with the rest of the cream.

Cover with plastic wrap, and refrigerate for at least 2 hours before serving.

When ready to serve, sprinkle with the cocoa or bits of grated chocolate.

This dessert will be even better if prepared the day before.

Serves 6–8
Prep time: 20 minutes
Refrigeration time:
at least 2 hours

4 egg yolks
5 tablespoons
  powdered sugar
1 pound mascarpone
½ cup crème fraîche
1 cup very strong coffee
½ cup amaretto (optional)
20 ladyfingers
  (at least 7 ounces)
Cocoa powder or
  grated chocolate

Serves 6
Prep time: 15 minutes
Cooking time: 15 minutes

6 cooking pears
1¼ cups red wine
Zest of ½ lemon
1 teaspoon vanilla
4 cloves
1 teaspoon
   ground cinnamon
5 ounces dried apricots
   (about 15 whole)
5 ounces raisins
   (1 cup, packed)
1¼ cups powdered sugar
3 ounces pine nuts

[fruits poached with wine and spices]

Peel the pears, keeping the stems on, and place in a saucepan with the wine, lemon zest, vanilla, spices, apricots, raisins and sugar. Bring to a boil, lower the heat, cover, and simmer for 15 minutes.

Let the pears cool in their cooking juice. With a slotted spoon, transfer pears to a compote dish, either whole or cut, lengthwise, in half. Add the pine nuts to the pan and reduce the juice to three-quarters, until it is like a syrup and slightly caramelized. Coat the pears with the juice. They can be served warm or cold, alone, or with a warm or chilled sabayon (see page 104).

[glossary]

Al dente: a term for cooking pasta until it is tender yet a bit firm to the bite. It should be tested frequently and drained immediately after it is ready.

Amaretti: little almond macaroons.

Arborio rice: Italians use it to make risotto. It is a big, long, round grain, which absorbs the broth without becoming sticky. Don't overcook or it will become soggy.

Asti spumante: Italian sparkling white wine from the Asti region.

Balsamic vinegar: Vinegar made from grape juice (not from wine) of the Modena region. It is light brown in color and full-bodied in flavor. It has little in common with other vinegars. It is frequently imitated so buy the imported product. Although the imported vinegar is more expensive, it is definitely better, and a little bit goes a long way.

Borlotti beans: big, dried white beans from Rome. They can be substituted with beans from Soisson.

Mascarpone: fresh cheese of creamy consistency, frequently used instead of cream.

Mozzarella: raw cheese, made from curdled milk, stretched in ribbons and twisted. The best kind, "buffala" (from buffalo milk) is expensive and is best enjoyed simply, with fresh tomatoes and a drizzle of extra virgin olive oil. The most common kind, "fior di latte" (from cow's milk), is used in cooked dishes.

Panettone: big, round bread (like a brioche) with raisins, candied fruits and citrus peel.

Parmesan cheese: the oldest and most famous of Italian cheeses. Its manufacture is strictly limited to the areas surrounding Parma, Reggio and Modena. That is why the best Parmesan is called "Parmigiano-Reggiano" after the names of the two cities where it has always been made. Buy it ungrated, and freshly grate it just before using.

Poivrades: small, purple colored tender artichokes with a delicate flavor. They are often sold in a bunch.

Ricotta: white cheese, drained fresh and made from cow's milk. Because of its consistency and nutty flavor, Italians use it in all kinds of recipes. In its place, either farmer's cheese or brousse cheese from Provence can be used.

Rocket (arugula): fresh little salad leaves with a peppery bite and taste. They are used alone or in a mesclun (mixture of salad greens), and can be purchased loose, by weight, in the market.

Vino santo: a Tuscan, sweet white wine.

[shopping advice]

It will not be difficult to find all the products needed in these recipes in local markets or Italian grocery stores. Nowadays, most markets have a variety of Italian products: Dried or semi fresh pasta, precooked polenta, dried tomatoes in oil—whole or puréed (often called "caviar of dried tomatoes")…and in the dairy category, ricotta, fresh mozzarella and mascarpone.

In produce markets, you will find fresh fruits and vegetables, as well as tomatoes from Sicily, baby spinach, mixed salad greens, arugula and fresh herbs. In an Italian grocery store, it will be easier to find Arborio rice for risotto, borlotti beans, dry Marsala or vino santo. There, also, the prosciutto and other pork products will be more authentic, and be sliced in the Italian manner. Don't hesitate to stock some spices and treat yourself to a good olive oil and quality balsamic vinegar for the seasoning of uncooked dishes—their flavor is unrivaled.

glossary

[index]

Published originally under the title Trattoria, ©2000 HACHETTE LIVRE (Hachette Pratique)

English translation for the U.S. market ©2001, Silverback Books, Inc.

Managing editors: Suyapa Audigier & Brigitte Éveno

Project editor: Lisa M. Tooker

Food editor: Terri Pischoff Wuerthner, CCP

Artwork and creation: Guylaine & Christophe Moi

Production: Nathalie Lautout & Patty Holden

Assistant editor: Sophie Brissaud

Editorial office: Sylvie Gauthier

Object photography: Matthieu Csech

Cover photo: Hoaqui/M. Renaudeau

Photos: page 10 Marco Polo/F. Bouillot, page 32 Sipa Press/Stumpf, page 52 Hoaqui/M. Renaudeau, page 74 Agence Ana/P. Horree, page 96 Sygma/G. Giansanti

Printed and bound in Singapore.

ISBN : 1-930603-36-3